Bad Shepherds

ROD BENNETT

BAD
SHEPHERDS

Times the Faithful Thrived
While Bishops Did
the Devil's Work

SOPHIA INSTITUTE PRESS
Manchester, New Hampshire

Copyright © 2018 by Rod Bennett

Printed in the United States of America. All rights reserved.

Cover design by Perceptions Design Studio.

On the cover: *Cardinals* (SEL244079) © 2005 by
Lincoln Seligman / Bridgeman Images.

Biblical references in this book are taken from the Catholic Edition of the
Revised Standard Version of the Bible, copyright 1965, 1966 by the Division
of Christian Education of the National Council of the Churches of Christ in
the United States of America. Used by permission. All rights reserved.

No part of this book may be reproduced, stored in a retrieval system, or trans-
mitted in any form, or by any means, electronic, mechanical, photocopying,
or otherwise, without the prior written permission of the publisher, except by
a reviewer, who may quote brief passages in a review.

Sophia Institute Press
Box 5284, Manchester, NH 03108
1-800-888-9344

www.SophiaInstitute.com

Sophia Institute Press® is a registered trademark of Sophia Institute.

Library of Congress Cataloging-in-Publication Data
To come

First printing

To Robert L. Ripley,
who gave me my first lessons in this sort of thing

I am the good shepherd. The good shepherd lays down his life for the sheep. He who is a hireling and not a shepherd, whose own the sheep are not, sees the wolf coming and leaves the sheep and flees; and the wolf snatches them and scatters them. He flees because he is a hireling and cares nothing for the sheep. I am the good shepherd; I know my own and my own know me, as the Father knows me, and I know the Father; and I lay down my life for the sheep.

— John 10:11–15

Contents

A Cautionary Note

This book, like most of my others, has a lot of history in it—but it isn't the work of a trained historian. I'm a history buff, a popularizer, someone whose gifts (if there are any) lie in the tricks of the storyteller's trade, a knack for making history interesting for people who don't usually like history. It's only too likely, in other words, that someone who really knows his stuff might stumble across a howler or two. My only plea? No one else seems to be doing this job for the Church right now—and as the great G. K. Chesterton once said, "A thing worth doing is worth doing badly."

Also, I'd be very sorry if anyone were to take this work as a veiled stab at any modern churchman not yet proved beyond a reasonable doubt to be guilty of wrongdoing. I have no trouble naming names such as Maciel, Law, and McCarrick; nor will I hesitate to pin my term "bad shepherd" on the tail of any donkey found guilty of malfeasance in the future. At the time of this writing, however, the jury is still out on many unsettled matters; and several popular candidates have been nominated for the title of "bad shepherd" though their guilt has not yet been proven. That being the case, I've stuck here, as I will continue to stick until compelled to do otherwise, to Pauline counsels on this subject:

Obey your leaders and submit to them, for they are keeping watch over your souls and will give an account. (Heb. 13:17)

Pay all of them their dues ... respect to whom respect is due, honor to whom honor is due. (Rom. 13:7)

Let the elders who rule well be considered worthy of double honor, especially those who labor in preaching and teaching.... Never admit any charge against an elder except on the evidence of two or three witnesses. (1 Tim. 5:17, 19)

Bad Shepherds

Introduction

When I was young and still a Baptist, my mother worked part-time as a secretary and librarian to a group of Evangelical clergymen in and around the city of Atlanta, Georgia. One day she both amused and shocked me by declaring that of these five or so distinguished ministers of the gospel, there had been only one who didn't end up being a challenge to her faith.

The first had shown himself crass and flirty with the ladies. Another locked the door of his comfortable office every afternoon for a "sweet hour of prayer"—which was actually a sweet hour (or three) of loud, comical snoring. The last had recently become famous on TV and thus acquired a towering Napoleonic ego, leaving his cringing staff to wonder when the Queen of Hearts was next going to holler, "Off with his head!"

The single happy exception had been one of the Queen of Hearts' lowly lieutenants. This meek little fellow spent most of his time visiting the sick and shut-ins, doing the grunt work his boss was now too good for, drawing scandalously little praise from the Big Man's flock, and seeking none. He died not long after my mom left his service, broke and disgraced—like his Master.

I hope nobody will imagine that I've written this book to contrast the sloth and hypocrisy of Protestant ministers with the superior unction and virtue of Catholic clergymen, my own shepherds since a 1996 conversion. I'm pretty sure, in fact—here in the wake of the calamitous revelations of 2018—that not many of my readers *will* jump quickly to that assumption, certainly not as quickly as they once might have done.

Ministers who end up being a challenge to one's faith have now become the Catholic problem par excellence, and the days when we could blithely brush off our scandals of abuse and cover-up as no worse than those of any other denomination are over (whatever modicum of truth that answer might once have contained).

In fact, I've far exceeded my mother's old record, having personally bumped up hard for years against one genuine clerical miscreant after another—not just the usual haughty heretics and all-too-obviously unchaste "celibates," but men whose misdeeds eventually forced even today's congenitally nonconfrontational authorities to return them (quietly) to a laicized state of life. Many of these personal experiences, if truth be told, were with strange, warped men who made my mom's bottom-pinching lothario and slumbering contemplative look like quaintly amusing characters in an episode of *The Andy Griffith Show*.

Looking back, I will say that my mom's memorable story gave me a mental category that really has helped through the years: "the shepherd who ends up being a challenge to your faith." It gave me a place to hang my hat, so to speak, during such days, a heads-up that prevented me from being caught off guard with no advance notice, much as St. Paul sought to provide for his own converts: "We would not have you ignorant, brethren" (1 Thess. 4:13); "Do not be deceived" (1 Cor. 15:33); "Understand this.... Men will [come] ... holding the form of religion but denying the power of it" (2 Tim. 3:1, 2, 5).

It's this kind of heads-up I'm hoping to provide in these pages, however postdated it may happen to be. For the Good

Shepherd has *always* been served, I'm afraid, by bad shepherds, ever since the days when His handpicked treasurer, a man who sat through every sermon in the Gospels, began helping himself to what was in the money box (see John 12:6). Judas Iscariot, as you may recall, was one of the Twelve Apostles designated to take the place of Judah or Benjamin, sitting on one of "twelve thrones" in the New Jerusalem and "judging the twelve tribes of Israel" (Matt. 19:28). And the office of an apostle is far higher in God's economy than a patriarch, a bishop, a cardinal—higher even than a pope. Yet Judas proved himself to be, in Christ's own words, "a devil" (John 6:70). Even true shepherds then, unambiguously designated as such by Christ, can be not just bad at times but downright diabolical—and worse than you think.

Most such notices move quickly at this point to the "Even so, the vast majority of our clergy are holy and good!" phase, with concerns about tarring the innocent along with the guilty; and though that interjection is certainly true and makes an important point, I'm going to let you wriggle on the hook a little more before moving on.

It's my conviction that if more of us realized just *how bad* our shepherds really can get—and have gotten throughout history —we might, for lack of surprise, be better fortified when these new Judases turn up in our day.

Babes in the woods often lose faith after discovering too suddenly that they've been wandering in a fool's paradise. In just the same way, many lifelong Catholics, lulled to sleep by the relative infrequency of bad shepherds like Benedict IX or Urban VI in recent times, may be too likely to *expect* their ministers to be living saints, rather than cherishing the saints for how precious and few such beings really are.

Under these conditions, we are prone to make *idols* of our shepherds; we may start treating them as a holy caste of spiritual aristocrats—and worse, training them to expect such treatment. Like the opera *prima donna* or the spoiled Broadway ham, they can start "believing their notices," rather than staying focused on earning them. And when some of these idols are exposed as having feet of clay, we'll all be a little less likely to lose our heads and go all apocalyptic if we've already "lived through" the Arian crisis of the fourth century or spent time with the urbane, ecclesiastical atheistic bad shepherds hovering 'round the court of Louis XIV.

It's a terrible subject, of course. I think of C. S. Lewis, who wrote the famous *Screwtape Letters*—thirty-one imaginary exchanges between two demons sharing with each other clever advice about how best to ensnare human victims. "Of all my books," Lewis confessed, "this was the only one I did not take pleasure in writing." Composing a whole volume written from the perspective of a tempter proved "dry and gritty work," he admitted, however valuable such a book might prove for training the faithful to recognize the devil's snares.

Similarly, I'd much rather have written (as I have done) about the saints and the champions, about heroes such as Justin and Ignatius, Antony and Athanasius, than about the poisonous rats who infest the pages ahead.

And I confess that I've worried a bit, in the writing of it, that a book like this might knock the wind out of somebody's sails out there—someone who might be considering the claims of the Catholic Church for the first time even in this very troubled hour of her life on earth. Or perhaps it might further distress the lifelong Catholic who is now tempted as never before to stop affiliating with this outfit that insists on making such an obvious spectacle of itself every night on the TV news.

Here's what kept me pressing ahead. When the archangel Gabriel announced the coming of Jesus our Savior, he told blessed mother Mary, "He will be great, and will be called the Son of the Most High; and the Lord God will give to him the throne of his father David" (Luke 1:31–33). We learn two neglected facts here: (1) that Jesus' new gospel kingdom is going to be God's Old Testament kingdom renewed and reborn; and (2) that all of us Christians are citizens of that endless kingdom, the house of Jacob; and even today Jesus sits on a throne that originally belonged to David, king of the Hebrews. All fine and good — but the more you know about the Hebrew kings who succeeded to that throne, the more astonishing these truths become. Out of thirty-nine kings all told, ruling over a kingdom divided into northern and southern parts, *thirty-one* were bad — several spectacularly so. Rehoboam, David's grandson, set up golden calves for the people to worship and deliberately caused the civil war his fathers always feared. Ahab persecuted the prophet Elijah and "sold himself to do what was evil in the sight of the LORD," urged on by his wife, Jezebel (1 Kings 21:25). Manasseh was a mass murderer who put an altar to Baal in Yahweh's Temple and later burned one of his sons there as sacrifice to Moloch.

Thirty-one out of thirty-nine — and this from a line of kings that God Himself had promised to "establish ... and make sure forever" (see 2 Sam 7:12–16). Certainly, our batting average in the Catholic Church is — at the very least, a bit higher than that. Of the total number of popes to date, for instance — 266 across a span of more than two thousand years — fewer than two dozen have been mixed up in serious wrongdoing. Meanwhile, more than 90 of them have been raised to the altar for exceptional sanctity; and there's no reason to think the proportions wouldn't be similar in a survey of all other clergy throughout the centuries.

BAD SHEPHERDS

The main point to gather, however, from the very unwholesome tale of the Davidic kings, is that wicked leaders ruling over God's flock, *with God's own sanction on their office* (but not on their actions), is an old, old story. It's also a profound mystery, of course, not unrelated to the mystery of Judas among the Twelve—but a profoundly biblical one. And if the bad popes and bad bishops prove, as I myself once believed, that the Catholic Church herself cannot have been established by God, then the very throne upon which our Savior sits cannot be of God, and the religion built around it must be false. I hope you will keep that mystery in mind as you review this similar, often unwholesome narrative.

Nevertheless, I don't think I'd have written at all if I hadn't quickly perceived a much more nourishing subplot running side by side with all the tragedy. My research, curiously enough, soon revealed *a major key running under the minor*; and this was the striking fact that the Catholic laity during the ages under review often shone brightest just when their bad shepherds were at their worst. God, in other words, had not left Himself without a witness. They not only survived but actually *thrived*, and their heroism finally turned the tide. And their victories were all the more glorious for having been won in spite of their leaders, rather than with their help. Soon it began to seem more and more likely to me that our crisis today, when it, too, becomes ancient history, will probably have ended in just the same remarkable way.

This is not just a history, then, but a history with a healing purpose, aimed at binding the wounds being inflicted on modern Catholics by their own bad shepherds. I've chosen to depict five eras, in particular, for this sketch: the Arian attempt to sell Christianity to the Roman emperors during the fourth century; the Dark Ages, which followed the fall of the empire, during which Christian bishops and popes too often became half-savage barbarians themselves; the idle and dissolute shepherds of the fourteenth and fifteenth centuries who delayed the universal cry for reform until it was too late; the Catholic rebels who started Protestantism in the sixteenth century and the men who drove them to it; and the French clergy who patriotically chose France over Christianity in the seventeenth and eighteenth centuries. And if these five examples afford us a vision of clergymen no better, at times, than Nero himself, they also show us a picture, equally important in this day and age, of ordinary Catholics who kept the Faith—for leaders who fiddled while Rome burned.

There's a proverb making the rounds these days: "When you're going through hell, keep on going." This book, likewise, seeks to take us *out* by taking us *farther in*. And with God's help, we may one day join the heroes who won their crowns by outlasting *the bad shepherds*.

> Men are never more awake to the good in the world than when they are furiously awake to the evil in the world. Men never enjoy so much the blazing sun and the rushing wind as when they are out hunting the Devil. On the other hand, there are no people so dreary as philosophical optimists; and men are never so little happy as when they are constantly reassured. Such men have begun by calling the moon as bright as the sun, but they end only by seeing the sun as pallid as the moon. They have made a shameful treaty with shame; and the mark of it is on them. Everything is good, except their own spirits."[1]

---

[1] G. K. Chesterton, *Illustrated London News*, December 16, 1905.

Chapter 1

Eyes Off the Prize:
The Arians of the Fourth Century

Arianism—the Church's direst *theological* crisis—happened early on. It happened, in fact, to the same generation that saw Christianity legalized under Constantine, and it brought about the first of our twenty-one great general councils, that of Nicaea. And though it certainly did take the form of a clash over theology, the colossal Arian crisis of the fourth century was not primarily, as in so many subsequent revolts, a contest between a conservative majority and an upstart group of young men with new ideas. Here, the bad shepherds weren't bad chiefly by being theological heretics—and we won't, incidentally, be defining a "bad shepherd" in this book purely as "someone on the outs with Church tradition."

No, what happened in the wake of the First Council of Nicaea was a hostile takeover attempt of the Church by duly ordained Catholic churchmen, using a theological novelty as a pretext for pursuing a set of entirely this-worldly ends. Called Arianism, it was a heresy weaponized against the existing Church of pre-Constantinian times, wielded by cynical, nontheological people for a wholly secular purpose—and the body count it left behind was all too literal and not metaphorical at all.

The revolt against the Church as she existed prior to Constantine *wasn't*, contrary to popular belief, made by the emperor himself or on his behalf. The First Council of Nicaea put down the theological novelty and did it decisively (by a vote of 311 to 2!), a result to which Constantine gave his own wholehearted sanction.

Arianism rose from its grave and came to real power only after Constantine's death, and—*The Da Vinci Code* notwithstanding—Nicaea's affirmations were solidly in line with majority Christian belief for the previous three centuries, as anyone at all familiar with the voluminous writings of the Ante-Nicene Church Fathers must concede. The theological side of the crisis, in fact, seems to have been precipitated by a brilliant little summation of the traditional view called *De Incarnatione* written by the precociously talented young ascetic Athanasius some ten years before Constantine ever got involved.

Here's what happened. During the third century since the Incarnation—the 200s—Christianity experienced such explosive growth, not only numerically but in popular esteem as well, that Christians were threatening to become a majority in the Roman Empire. Christ's sun was rising everywhere, and just when that of the moribund old Roman paganism had begun to enter its final sunset. This meant that Christianity passed through a dangerous phase when it was *about as strong* as the forces of anti-Christianity, a good old-fashioned Mexican standoff, as they say. When the emperor himself jumped on the bandwagon, however (in A.D. 311), the scales shifted alarmingly. And though Constantine never did make Christianity the official religion of the empire (contrary, once again, to popular belief), he did hitch his hopes for Roman renewal to the vibrant new movement and gave it every unofficial and quasi-official sanction he could. Those who, for whatever reason, felt disinclined to join him in the Church needed some way to survive and prosper under the new conditions—and their pressing demand gradually began to create its own supply *within the Catholic episcopate.*

Arius of Alexandria, for whom the heresy is named, was a Catholic theologian himself, a priest in Roman Egypt. Young Athanasius had even been one of his deacons. A proud man, who gradually allowed his rationalistic bent to run well ahead of his judgment, Arius went off the rails by demanding that traditional beliefs about the divinity of Christ be squared with his own idea of strict monotheism. Arius stumbled, in other words, over what would later be called the mystery of the Holy Trinity. It isn't quite right to say, as you often hear, that Arians denied the divinity of Christ. No, they were always very ready to ascribe to Him every single godly honorific—all holy, all wise, all knowing, Creator of the universe—every single divine attribute but one: that of being fully co-eternal with His Father. Arius's favorite catchphrase captures the gist of the heresy: "There was a time when the Son was not." In Arius's system, the Second Person is a created being Himself, a kind of Xerox copy of God, perfect in every way, to be sure, but not, as in orthodox belief, consubstantial with His Father from all eternity. All this to solve Arius's personal problems with the notion of a Divine Son, truly distinct from His Father, who is, nevertheless, *not* a second God.

Arius died not long after making a cranky, tone-deaf speech on behalf of his scheme to the frowning delegates at Nicaea —right at the start of the affair, in other words. The actual heresiarch, then, wasn't the real head of the Arian heresy, and even the Arianism he invented got lost somewhere along the way, modified beyond recognition over the next five decades by the political exigencies of the moment. The only reason Arianism is remembered at all is that certain political figures chose that system and conspired with certain Christian clergymen to get it tolerated — and then mainstreamed — within the Catholic fold.

For what reason?

Because Arianism, ostensibly Christian though it was, was flexible enough and similar enough to certain brands of existing paganism to provide a refuge within the new order for unreconstructed Roman heathens. Jupiter, after all, king of the gods of the Romans, had sired half-human sons himself — Perseus, Apollo, and Hercules — and a Christian "Son of God" in some similar sense might be a person to whom the pagans could swear allegiance without stepping too far out of their accustomed thought forms. Arianism was, in essence, the rump of Roman paganism trying to survive in a Christian-flavored form. As such, it was highly attractive to social engineers on both sides of the divide.

From the secular point of view, Arianism would ease the transition for the non-Christian population, allowing them to accept baptism and to avow themselves Christian (in some sense) during an era when anything like true separation of church and state had yet to be invented.

From the Christian point of view, so called, Arianism might help to ensure that Constantine's bold gambit would *succeed permanently*. Lacking our historical hindsight, it was easy for our forebears to worry that Constantine might be replaced someday by another, more traditional (i.e., pagan) Roman emperor who might very well undertake simply to undo everything his predecessor had accomplished along these lines — and even renew the bloody persecutions to which Constantine had put a stop.

Very well: if Arius wasn't the driving force behind Arianism, who was? Later events prove that the man behind the curtain all along—the shrewd mind behind Arius's bookish one, the popularizer of Arius, Huxley to his Darwin—was a slippery master of intrigue named Eusebius of Nicomedia (not to be confused with his more famous contemporary, Eusebius of Caesarea, author of the well-known *Ecclesiastical History*). Eusebius, who was censured for Arianism at the Council of Nicaea but later wriggled off the hook, was bishop of Constantinople, the empire's eastern capital at the time. He used his friendship with the emperor's sister Constantia to ingratiate himself into Constantine's household, installing one of his own creatures as the empress's chaplain, a priest "tinctured with the dogmas of Arianism."[2]

Gradually, Eusebius was able to convince many influential people at court that the whole case against Arius and his beliefs had been a misunderstanding all along and that the heresiarch had been unjustly condemned. Soon, Arian clergymen began to be rehabilitated and then promoted within the Church by their powerful friends. The emperor himself resisted these pressures, never actually repudiating the decrees of Nicaea, but he did waffle on the subject more than a little, especially later in his life, when the council's lopsided 311–2 ratio drew steadily closer and closer to 50–50—and beyond.

His eldest son, Constantius, however, had no memories of Christianity as it had previously existed or allegiance to it. He saw only two groups of squabbling partisans within the Church, roughly equal in numbers by this point: one very eager to aid the empire in achieving her political goals of unity and domestic tranquility; the other anxious to demand, as fathers in the Faith, the emperor's submission to their particular brand of orthodoxy.

---

[2] Socrates Scholasticus, *Ecclesiastical History*, I:24.

So, when Constantine died in 337 and Constantius rose to the purple in his place, the new emperor hesitated in this matter hardly at all. He began actively promoting the Arian cause right away, using all the power and prestige of his mighty office, opening the gates of the Catholic Church to a literally unprecedented wave of heretical infiltration.

Make no mistake: these Arians were by no means Catholics in their faith, even though they absolutely were full-fledged, regularly ordained Catholic bishops and priests. They were, to put it shortly, *collaborators*—like the Catholic clergy (a minority, to be sure, though not a small one) who signed on to Adolf Hitler's program for a de-Judaified Christianity in twentieth-century Germany. They actively collaborated with Constantius in his effort to smooth the way for millions of insincere baptisms and for a watered-down Catholicism that might be counted on to "play ball" with the Roman state.

And this illustrates very well the danger of a clergy that takes its eyes off the next world and begins focusing on this one. St. Paul, in recommending celibacy, does so on just this basis: because a "married man is anxious about worldly affairs, how to please his wife, and his interests are divided," while "the unmarried man is anxious about the affairs of the Lord, how to please the Lord" (1 Cor. 7:32–34). His principle, however, extends well beyond celibacy to all other aspects of the clerical vocation: "I want you to be free from anxieties." The Catholic shepherd has just one job: to get his flock safely past the snares of this wilderness we live in and bring them in the end to the peace and security of their Father's house.

These Arian quislings, these bad shepherds, alas, took their eyes off this one job and *divided their attention*—how to stay on good terms with the surrounding culture, how to gain influence in government, how to avoid future persecution, how to secure for themselves a comfortable living. They became the new Pharisees: those clerics of the Old Testament "church" who sought to suppress reports of Christ's many miracles because, "if we let him go on thus, every one will believe in him, and the Romans will come and destroy both our holy place and our nation" (John 11:48). Trying to keep too many balls in the air at once, those bishops and priests who joined up with Eusebius ended up dropping the only one that really mattered.

At first, Arian efforts within the Church had been subtle, or rather, devious. The initial phase of their program had been an effort to replace the creed of Nicaea with something less clear-cut, more ambiguous, something everyone could agree on. A half dozen or more new creeds were contrived; and the Arians strove mightily to make them sound as close to orthodoxy as possible while leaving just enough wiggle room for an Arian interpretation. The Son, for instance, rather than being consubstantial with His Father, is "like his Father" and "in complete union with his Father." "When the Arians began this policy of verbal compromise," writes Catholic historian Hilaire Belloc,

> the Emperor Constantine and his successors regarded that policy as an honest opportunity for reconciliation and reunion. The refusal of the Catholics to be deceived became, in the eyes of those who thought thus, mere obstinacy; and in the eyes of the Emperor, factious rebellion and inexcusable disobedience. "Here are you people, who call yourself the only real Catholics, prolonging and needlessly embittering a mere faction-fight.... Such arrogance is intolerable. The other side have accepted your

main point [the divinity of Christ]; why cannot you now settle the quarrel and come together again? By holding out you split society into two camps; you disturb the peace of the Empire and are as criminal as you are fanatical." That is what the official world tended to put forward and honestly believed. The Catholics answered: "The heretics have *not* accepted our main point. They have subscribed to an Orthodox phrase, but they interpret that phrase in an heretical fashion. They will repeat that Our Lord is of Divine nature, but *not* that He is fully God, for they still say He was created. Therefore we will not allow them to enter our communion. To do so would be to endanger the vital principle by which the Church exists, the principle of the Incarnation, and the Church is essential to the Empire and Mankind."[3]

Before long, Constantius began to treat resistance to his religious policy as out-and-out mutiny. Already, Eustathius, bishop of Antioch, the man who wielded the gavel at Nicaea, had been railroaded into retirement by means of some transparently bogus accusations of immorality that his own flock knew very well to be false. Now Constantius felt free to replace Paul, the orthodox patriarch of Constantinople, with Eusebius of Nicomedia himself. Not long after that, he exiled Athanasius (a hero now in the eyes of the laity for his debates against Arius at the council and for his courageous stand ever since) from his see at Alexandria and replaced him with an Arian, too—again, on trumped-up charges that deceived no one. Gradually, in similar fashion, all the great

---

[3] Hilaire Belloc, *The Great Heresies* (Charlotte, NC: TAN Books, 1991), 30.

bishoprics of the Christian East—Ephesus, Ancyra, Hadrianople, Heraclea—were filled with Christological heretics.

Here is the point, however, at which God's lowly laity began to shine. The simple, dutiful man or woman in the pew was never, in any great numbers, at all fooled by any of this. The truth of the matter had been plain to them from the beginning: Arianism was a political scheme dreamed up by politicians for purposes of their own; nothing more, nothing less. Laypeople were the guinea pigs; Constantius and his ilk were the experimenters.

Yes, most of these ordinary Joes and Josephines knew very well that they were likely to get the short end in any debate over theology; Arian controversialists were, according to Cardinal John Henry Newman, extremely clever, but, "destitute of religious seriousness and earnestness ... they engaged in theological discussion as a mere trial of skill or as a literary recreation." But laypeople also knew very well who still talked like a Christian and who had *something else* in their voice. Athanasius (who took refuge at this time with Pope Julius of Rome) witnessed their fidelity firsthand on his long walk out of town, greeted by great outpourings of popular enthusiasm all along the way. "'Subscribe [to Arian doctrine] or withdraw from your churches!' the emperor commanded.... It was only in this way that Constantius forced so great a multitude of Bishops [to give in]," Athanasius would later report. "They were allowed no relief, not even permitted to go out of their dwellings until they had either subscribed, or refused and incurred banishment. And he did this because he saw that the heresy was hateful to all men. It was for this reason that he compelled so many to add their names to the small number of Arians.... Yet even so, most men have remained faithful."[4]

---

[4] Athanasius, *History of the Arians*, IV:32.

His flock at Alexandria balked when they got the news that Athanasius was to be replaced by a handpicked party man. Never, they avowed—no, never! And so the new Arian bishop of Alexandria—one Gregory of Cappadocia—marched into the city surrounded by a cohort of five thousand troops. The orthodox population was brushed out of the way with all the gentleness you would expect from hardened Roman campaigners. Priests and deacons who stayed loyal to their true bishop were hunted out and abused, churches desecrated, holy vessels overturned, religious sisters raped. This "rioting" Constantius used as an excuse for further repressions. He regretted the violence, of course, but law and order must obviously be restored.

Athanasius stayed three years in the Christian West, where Arianism had yet to gain a foothold. Reports from his home diocese must have made him frantic to return—which remained wholly impossible:

> [Gregory] accuses before the governor those who pray in their own homes; and he takes every opportunity to insult their ministers. His conduct is of such violence, then, that many run the risk of going unbaptized, and many have no one to visit them in sickness and distress, a circumstance which they regret more bitterly than their illness. For while the ministers of the Church are under persecution, the people condemn the impiety of the Arian heretics, and choose rather to be sick and to run the risk, than to permit the hand of the Arians to come upon their head.[5]

---

[5] Athanasius, in William A. Jurgens, *Faith of the Early Fathers* (Collegeville, MN: Liturgical Press, 1979), 322.

Peaceful though this form of resistance might be, Constantius treated it as contempt for his authority. He sent into the streets gangs armed with swords and clubs, to disrupt orthodox prayer services, casting "defrocked" clergy into prison, starving them while there, and dragging holy women away by the hair. Later, the bishops of Alexandria achieved "compliance" from their flock by imitating a method first used by the Arian Macedonius at Constantinople:

> Many persons eminent for their piety were seized and tortured, because they refused to communicate with [an Arian bishop]: and after the torture, they forcibly constrained the men to be partakers of the holy mysteries, their mouths being forced open with a piece of wood, and then the consecrated elements thrust into them. Those who were so treated regarded this as a punishment far more grievous than all others.

Meantime, Pope Julius summoned a synod of impartial Western bishops to investigate the charges against Athanasius. This synod, of course, had little difficulty exonerating him completely, whereupon the pontiff protested to the emperor's lackeys back in Byzantium Athanasius's removal. He reminded them that any action against Athanasius

> should have been according to the established ecclesiastical canon … [that they should have] written to us, so that the justice of it might be seen as emanating from all.… If any suspicion had rested upon the bishop there, notice of it ought to have been written to the Church here. But now, after they have done as they pleased [by substituting Gregory for Athanasius at Alexandria] they want to obtain

our concurrence, although we never condemned him.…
This is a novel form of procedure.[6]

The Eusebians (as Athanasius often called the Arian party,
emphasizing his belief that their theological hang-ups were only
a pretext) responded by conducting another council of their
own, the Council of Antioch in 341. This dog-and-pony show
accomplished little besides the framing of a series of decrees aimed
solely at preventing Athanasius from returning to his rightful
see. One of these was a straight-up sentence of death upon the
patriarch *in absentia*, confirmed by the emperor, to be carried out
the moment he dared step back into Egypt.

Soon, outright civil war erupted in several places. The historian Socrates gives the example of a group in Paphlagonia (on
the southern shore of the Black Sea) that was "put to flight in all
directions" when the Arian bishop of Cyzicus ordered the complete destruction of any church "maintaining the doctrine of con-
substantiality." The same kind of torments employed elsewhere
were resorted to, along with a new level of horror involving sexual
torture of females. Finally, "Macedonius caused, by the emperor's
permission, four companies of soldiers to be sent into Paphlagonia,
that through dread of the military the people might receive the
Arian opinion." This is how, finally, the original, peaceful population of the region was goaded into taking up arms.

> Animated to desperation by zeal for their religion, they
> armed themselves with long reap-hooks, hatchets, and
> whatever weapon came to hand, and went forth to meet
> the troops; on which a conflict ensuing, many indeed of
> the Paphlagonians were slain, but nearly all the soldiers

[6] Pope Julius, in Jurgens, *Faith of the Early Fathers*, 346.

were destroyed.... Such were the exploits of Macedonius on behalf of Christianity, consisting of murders, battles, incarcerations, and civil wars: proceedings which rendered him odious not only to the objects of his persecution, but even to his own party.[7]

Shocked by such losses and embarrassed, now, by Julius's letter and by the charge that hatred for Athanasius and the other Nicene champions was primarily an Eastern phenomenon, Eusebius and Constantius realized that they must turn their sights on Rome itself and the bishops of the West. Clearly, the only way Arianism would ever be accepted everywhere, without the need for violent military suppression and the enormous costs associated with it, was to seize the papacy and impose Arius's system from the top down.

To this end, Constantius called yet another council, but a Western council this time, to be held in Italy. This was the Council of Milan, which took place in the spring of 355. All the Western bishops were invited, of course, but the galleries were also heavily packed with Eastern delegates whose travel expenses had, of course, been paid for out of the imperial treasury. Constantius showed up as well, though he listened in on the proceedings from a curtained antechamber. Another creed was drawn up, orthodox on the face of it, but minus the all-important word *consubstantial*. "Those who," according to Newman, "would rather have suffered death than have sanctioned the impieties of Arius, hardly saw how to defend themselves in refusing creeds which were abstractedly true, though incomplete, and intolerable only because [they were] the badges of a prevaricating party."[8]

---

[7] Socrates Scholasticus, *Ecclesiastical History*, II:38.
[8] John Henry Newman, *Arians of the Fourth Century* (Notre Dame, IN: University of Notre Dame Press, 2001), 144.

Most signed under the circumstances—circumstances not, we're forced to admit, unrelated to the large number of Roman troops encircling the council hall.

But when another set of phony charges against Athanasius was produced as well, nearly half the assembly drew the line; at which point the Roman emperor rushed from behind his curtain, brandishing a sword, nearly apoplectic with rage. He flatly ordered every man to sign or face the consequences. And at this point, you will be pleased to hear, most of the Western prelates cowboyed up well enough:

> When the bishops heard this they were utterly amazed, and stretching forth their hands to God, they used great boldness of speech against him, teaching him that the kingdom was not his but God's, who had given it to him, Whom also they bid him fear, lest He should suddenly take it away from him. And they threatened him with the day of judgment and warned him against infringing ecclesiastical order and mingling Roman sovereignty with the constitution of the Church and introducing the Arian heresy into the Church of God. But he would not listen to them, nor permit them to speak further, but threatened them so much the more.[9]

After obtaining the signatures of the entire Eastern delegation, along with those of a good many Westerners, Constantius banished another 147 bishops—solely for refusing a guilty verdict on Athanasius, which the emperor found politically expedient. Even Dionysius, the bishop in whose cathedral the council was held,

---

[9] Athanasius, *History of the Arians*, IV:34.

was exiled from the Roman Empire with the approval, whether active or tacit, of over 300 of his brother bishops.

When one of his deacons, Hilarius, protested too loudly, he was stripped, tied to a pillar in the sight of all, and flogged half to death.

> The deacon, while he was being scourged, praised the Lord, remembering His words, "I gave my back to the smiters [Isa. 50:6]," but they, while they scourged him, laughed and mocked him, feeling no shame that they were insulting a Levite. Indeed, they acted but consistently in laughing while he continued to praise God; for it is the part of Christians to endure stripes, but to scourge Christians is the outrage of a Pilate or a Caiaphas.[10]

Here again we must emphasize that these Arians were *not* men of another religion, another tribe, aliens to the Christian Faith; indeed, many of the bishops who rubber-stamped Constantius's edicts at Milan had been present at the First Council of Nicaea—and were thus among the 311 who voted up the word *consubstantial* in the first place!

The pope was likewise imprisoned—not by an emperor, as was Peter under Nero, nor by a dictator, as was Pius VI by Napoleon—but by other Catholic bishops whose ordination was as valid as his own. The pope to which we refer was Liberius, who became bishop of Rome in April of 352 upon the death of Athanasius's old friend Julius. When attempts to bribe him failed, Liberius was simply arrested and deposed. He was carried away to what is today Bulgaria and held in a dungeon. One of his deacons, Felix, was, on the emperor's orders, consecrated to

---

[10] Ibid., V:41.

replace Liberius—after being hastily created a bishop at the hands of another clutch of turncoats.

Felix, we must say, was a very reluctant antipope. He never embraced Arianism, but he did celebrate the Mass together with Arian clergy, apparently under the "can't we all just get along?" delusion that has so often been the excuse for episcopal timidity. "He preserved inviolate the doctrines set forth in the Nicene confession of faith," concedes Theodoret the historian, "yet he held communion with those who had corrupted that faith. For this reason none of the citizens of Rome would enter the House of Prayer while he was in it."[11] Once again, the laity shone—at a time when clerical spines needed stiffening badly.

While Liberius was being softened up, another great Nicene hero was arrested: Hosius of Cordoba, a dear friend of Constantius's father, and the foremost Western bishop besides the pope. He, too, was chained and shackled in an unheated cell during the dead of winter, fed only sporadically, awakened in the middle of the night and threatened with tortures unless he should "see the light" on the Arian question. These reports drew the harshest condemnation ever to fall from the pen of the great Athanasius: "Godless, unholy, without natural affection," he wrote in describing Constantius,

> he feared not God, he regarded not his father's affection for Hosius, he reverenced not his great age [close to one hundred by this point!].... All of these things this modern Ahab, this second Belshazzar of our times, disregarded for the sake of impiety. He used such violence toward the old

---

[11] Theodoret, *Ecclesiastical History*, II:14.

man, and confined him so tightly, that at last, broken by suffering, he was brought, though hardly, to hold communion with Valens, Ursacius, and their fellows, though he would not subscribe against Athanasius. Yet even thus he forgot not his duty, for at the approach of death, as it were by his last testament, he bore witness to the force which had been used towards him, and anathematized the Arian heresy, and gave strict charge that no one should receive it.[12]

Liberius seems to have been broken in a similar manner about the same time (though to what degree has always been a matter of debate). Anti-Catholics have always used his supposed fall as an argument against papal infallibility, but the story is of no use at all for that purpose. Everyone agrees that at the very worst, Liberius signed the Semi-Arian Creed of Sirmium, a document, like so many others, that had been deliberately designed to bear both an orthodox and a heretical interpretation. The Church teaches that the pope's gift of infallibility is in play only when he gives an official definition of doctrine, with the expressed intent that it should be binding upon the whole Church—and he must act freely, *without coercion*, leaving Liberius's act, whatever it was, entirely outside of the question.

The promise, in other words, is a promise of *infallibility* to Peter's successor as a transmitter of apostolic doctrine under certain narrowly defined conditions, not (as we will soon see quite vividly) a promise of *impeccability* (personal sinlessness, that is, or the inability to stumble or make mistakes in more routine circumstances).

---

[12] Athanasius, *History of the Arians*, V:46.

Most interesting as well: Constantius never crowed over the pope's supposed fall, and Liberius never issued any Arian decrees after his return to Rome (which had, of course, been the whole point).

The Arian historian Philostorgius says nothing about any fall but does tell us that the Romans rose up and kicked the antipope Felix out, obliging the emperor to release Liberius for fear of another sanguine uprising. This, it would seem, ought to be enough to counter the admittedly curious fact that even Athanasius appears to have believed reports that the pope finally gave in, as Hosius did, purely out of fear and exhaustion.

Speaking of Athanasius, he, too, was nearly captured and put to death in the horrible winter of 355. He had, through a series of circumstances too complicated to recount here, managed to return more than once to his home church at Alexandria (he was, by the way, exiled by four emperors no fewer than *five times!*). At this point, however, he was so firmly fixed in the public mind as the veritable figure of *orthodoxy incarnate* that Constantius had feared to attack him directly. But he did set a trap for him by encouraging him to say Mass in an as-yet-unconsecrated basilica (a breach of Church law). Had Athanasius fallen for it, this act would have been used, once again, as an excuse for his removal. The patriarch was too wily for the emperor this time, however; changing his plans at the last minute, he celebrated the holy day in question at another church. Infuriated, the local authorities attempted to arrest him there anyway, without any pretext. Athanasius narrowly escaped, in circumstances that seemed almost miraculous to his orthodox "fans," and he disappeared, once again, into the desert. He was quickly replaced, of course, by another rank heretic.

Here, finally, the bottom was reached — perhaps the closest the Catholic Church has ever come to being overthrown, to becoming an apostate body. Historians tell us that probably *eight out of ten Catholic bishoprics worldwide* were, at this point, in the hands of counterfeit Christians. Another historian asserts that the number of episcopal sees that can be shown to have remained in orthodox hands throughout the crisis can be counted *on the fingers of one hand.*

The Nicene Fathers had all either fled, been compromised, been imprisoned, or apostatized themselves and joined the enemy. An antipope sat upon the chair of Peter and Athanasius, the little man whose little book may have started the whole war, huddled in a cave in the Thebaid desert, sheltered by hermits and goatherds.

In short, orthodox Christian clergy were an endangered species, and this was as close as they have ever come to final extinction. This is that terrible time of which St. Jerome later spoke, when he wrote his famous words *Ingemuit totus or bis et Arianum se esse miratus est* — "The whole world groaned and was astonished to find itself Arian."

And yet the laity—the blessed laity—now sheep without a shepherd, as it were, once again, prayed their prayers, worked their works of compassion, continued their patient imitation of Christ … and kept on keeping on. They sheltered the heroes, shunned the traitors, protested the novelties, shed their blood when they had to, and clung tenaciously to "the faith which was once for all delivered to the saints" (Jude 1:3). And they waited for the coming of spring.

It did finally come, of course—just as it always does. It's far too long a story to tell here, but Arianism collapsed of its own weight only a few years later. At the very peak of his power, Constantius fell to another claimant, his nephew Julian. Raised by Arians from his youth, Julian hated and despised the very sound of Arianism—but, alas, of orthodoxy as well.

Julian is the Caesar whom the Arians (and their more moderate sympathizers, the Semi-Arians) always dreaded, the man for fear of whom they had, whether consciously or otherwise, committed every outrage: the Caesar who went back to paganism. Known to history as Julian the Apostate, this is the man who attempted to undo what Constantine (his great-uncle) had done. Julian, at least at first, didn't begin persecuting Christianity, didn't even outlaw it or end the policy of toleration. No, his initial strategy was to let the Arians and the Orthodox continue undermining their own religion with their "everlasting war over words," believing they would finally tear each other to pieces, allowing paganism to rise again by default.

Either way, his schemes quickly came to nothing; Julian was killed on a battlefield in Persia less than three years after taking office. And though more than one Arian emperor—the spiritual successors of Constantius—followed him over the next decade, the thing dried up because Julian had put the fear of God in everyone (quite against his own will, of course). The cowardly attempt at "peace through subservience to secular authority" had failed: the anti-Constantine had arisen anyway. Likewise, "many Semi-Arians, disgusted by the excesses of the extreme Arian party and frightened by the appearance of an apostate on the throne, returned to the unity of the Church." When that moment came, the whole thing blew over (at least inside the empire) about as quickly as the storm had blown up to begin with.

Cowardice is the key word. Everything done by these bad shepherds had been done in contradiction to our Lord's edict in the glorious Sermon on the Mount: "Do not be anxious about your life ... saying, 'What shall we eat?' or 'What shall we drink?' or 'What shall we wear?'.... But seek first his kingdom and his righteousness, and all these things shall be yours as well"

(Matt. 6:25, 31, 33). Every horror to which the Arian party descended—practically all Arians, mind you, Catholic priests and bishops *acting against their own brethren*—was occasioned by fear. Even worse, it was occasioned by fear of losing, as they say, "the lifestyle to which they had become accustomed."

Lesson learned?

St. Paul gives it once again, to our clergy today and to us laypeople as well: "Be watchful, stand firm in your faith, be courageous, be strong" (1 Cor. 16:13).

And keep your eyes on the prize.

Chapter 2

The Age of Iron:
Barbarian Bishops of the Dark Ages

The Church's relationship with the Roman Empire was ... well, complicated.

Though she was violently persecuted by the emperors at times—ten times under the pagan Caesars and then afterward, as we have seen, under Arian and other ostensibly Christian regimes—her association with the empire had good points as well. Roman stability, the vast network of Roman roads, the common language shared by all literate men (which was Greek, at first, inherited from Alexander the Great and spread by his Roman inheritors) all helped to create that Christian "population explosion" that brought Constantine to power. The Christian Gospels are written in that common language, and the Catholic Mass soon came to be said everywhere in the Latin tongue of Tertullian, Hippolytus, and Augustine.

The cosmopolitan nature of the empire, uniting as it did dozens of diverse tribes and populations into one strong, relatively enlightened family of nations, kept Christianity from becoming too narrowly associated with any one race or ethnicity, especially in the days when the empire included not just Europe but Western Asia, the Middle East, and North Africa. Once converted, the

Romans undertook vast missionary endeavors, charitable works, and the building of churches, orphanages, and hospitals in the name of Christ, often at imperial expense.

Mainly, Rome offered peace: a commodity that was always cherished by her people, though, in order to secure it, they maintained the greatest military force the world had ever known. To put it simply, her legions *kept out the surrounding chaos* and made a gigantic safe space for civilization—a safe space for commerce, the rule of law, and for prosperity, which the surrounding barbarians constantly regarded with envious eyes.

Some two hundred years after the reign of Julian the Apostate, that Roman Empire fell. Yes, those barbarians did rush the gates eventually, and they took what they had always wanted, but only after many decades of rust and decay, of laziness and luxury, of bills unpaid and virtues gone to seed. "For five or six hundred years," as Belloc puts it, "men carved less well, wrote verse less well, let roads fall slowly into ruin, lost or rather coarsened the machinery of government, forgot or neglected much in letters and in the arts and in the sciences."[13] The tottering walls became too expensive to defend—the northern frontier against the Germanic tribes, the eastern frontier against the Huns and the Visigoths in Russia, the multitudinous garrisons on the lower Rhine keeping out the Franks—forcing taxes within the empire to intolerable levels. By the end, when the Romans themselves had gotten too soft to sign up anymore, recruiters were filling military billets with men invited across the borders *from these very exterior tribes*—men who, not too surprisingly, practically welcomed their cousins in with open arms when the time came.

[13] Hilaire Belloc, *Europe and the Faith* (Charlotte, NC: TAN Books, 1991), 49.

The last blow was struck by the Ostrogoths, rushing in from the steppes of southern Russia. And when the whole enormous edifice finally did come down, the Dark Ages began.

The period that followed—from, say, 552 or so, to the First Council of the Lateran, in 1123—may be profitably thought of as the age of the *postapocalyptic Church*. Movie fans are familiar with the genre, which includes popular titles such as *Escape from New York*, *Waterworld*, and the *Mad Max* films. The famous Catholic historian Baronius coined a term for this period of Church history that sounds just like another entry in the same category: the *Age of Iron*. If you've seen some of those movies, you can perhaps imagine what a postapocalyptic Christianity might look like, and what you imagine (minus the sci-fi elements, of course) wouldn't be far wrong. "The cities are depopulated, the monasteries ruined and burned, the country reduced to solitude," lamented a synod of bishops, writing at a time near the low point.

> Just as the first men lived without law or fear of God, abandoned to their passions, so now every man does what seems good in his own eyes, despising laws human and divine and the commands of the Church. The strong oppress the weak; the world is full of violence against the poor and of the plunder of ecclesiastical goods.... Men devour one another like fishes in the sea.[14]

Needless to say, the bad shepherds returned with a vengeance as well. In fact, this is the period of Catholic history from which Martin Luther and the other Protestant Reformers drew some

---

[14] Christopher Dawson, *The Making of Europe* (New York: Macmillan), 266–267.

of their juiciest horror stories, their most effective anti-Catholic propaganda.

Before moving on, we need to finesse the term *fall of the Roman Empire* a little. What fell was the *western half* of Constantine's once-united empire—not the entire empire. After his reign, it was split in two, just as it had been a few decades before Constantine reunited it, and it remained split until the end. The eastern half, much the richer portion by this time, was centered around the new capital at Constantinople (a city once known as Byzantium on the straits of the Bosporus).

This eastern portion, where practically the entire drama of our previous chapter took place, remained standing, remained independent, and remained recognizably Roman long after old Rome on the Tiber had fallen to the Vandal hordes. In fact, it maintained its claim of continuity with the Caesars until just a few years before Columbus discovered America! This is the portion historians have come to refer to as the *Byzantine Empire*.

But even the part that *did* fall may not have fallen exactly as it does in the popular imagination. The barbarians who poured in were less interested in wiping out than in taking over. Those foreign recruits we mentioned intermingled with the invaders themselves, who wanted to see not the end of the empire but themselves enjoying its benefits.

So what really "fell" in the long run was *central control over the western portion of Roman Empire*, after which the generals and the former military governors of its various administrative districts gradually became the rulers of new, independent nations. Indeed, the old European titles of nobility—king, duke, count, and so forth—have all evolved from previous rankings in the Roman army: *rex, dux, comte,* and the like. All these ruled for a while in the name of the shadowy, half-remembered emperor of

Byzantium far away—but Byzantium itself made little effort to exert authority over its collapsing western reaches and offered no active support or succor at all.

Meanwhile, bad shepherds around the fringes of the empire sowed the seeds of future trouble. Lingering Arianism (and other Christological heresies) in places beyond the Christian emperor's reach—places such as the Arabian Peninsula—set the stage for tragedies to come. The Arabia into which the simple camel trader Muhammad was born in 571 had a religious population divided roughly into thirds: one-third pagans, one-third Jews, and one-third Arians and the like—with practically no orthodox Christians. The Christianity, then, that Muhammad came to reject so dramatically was really the same toxic concoction that had tried to kill the empire from within two centuries before.

The Prophet of Islam simply took Arian difficulties about the Trinity to their logical conclusion by denying the divinity of Christ altogether (while keeping, nevertheless, a high role for Jesus as a merely human prophet like Moses). When his successors carried the new message into the southern and far-eastern sections of the empire, they found whole nations similarly weakened by *bad Christianity*—not just heretical at times but also undermined by entrenched abuses that even the Catholic authorities showed little haste to reform.

Slavery, for instance (which had been the economic basis of the empire for centuries), had been allowed to continue deep into the Christian era with very little protest—far longer, in other words, than it was allowed to remain in America. It's true that it was gradually weakening in the sunshine of the Christian worldview—freeing one's slaves, for instance, had always been considered a laudable, *voluntary* work of mercy—but the institution was still nearly omnipresent inside the empire of the fifth and sixth centuries. Many bishops and priests (probably popes as well) were slaveholders themselves. Catholic clergymen were too often high-livers in other ways, also, and at a time when the laity were crushed by rampant usury and impossibly high taxation.

The armies of the Prophet, on the other hand, brought instant liberation wherever their message was accepted, for Islam prohibited any Muslim from taking usury or keeping a slave. By 750, at any rate, Islam had, by a remarkable combination of conversion and conquest, replaced Christianity in North Africa, in most of western Asia, and even in Spain in the Roman West —leaving only the Byzantine portions of the old empire still under the control of Christian Rome.

By the beginning of the sixth century, Arian outsiders were infiltrating what had been the Western Roman Empire as well. One group, in particular, the Lombards, migrated south from still-pagan Scandinavia and eventually gained control of Italy. Other Arian groups captured the west bank of the Rhine and the northern half of Gaul, and everywhere they went, they persecuted Catholics and suppressed orthodox churches. One of the Franks, however, a rough, warlike chieftain named Clovis, happened to fall for Clotilda, the Catholic princess of Gaul, and Clovis, happily, was no Arian but still a straight-up, unbaptized heathen. Providentially, he allowed himself to be converted by Catholics, whereupon three thousand of his countrymen asked for baptism as well. This not only gave the Western Christians an ally and a protector but also wound up planting Catholic Christianity firmly in the rich soil that became France, the rock-solid center of Christendom for the next thousand years.

There were other Catholic victories during these centuries, to be sure. Pope St. Gregory the Great sent missionaries to convert the English. Irish missionaries, the spiritual sons of St. Patrick, took the Faith to Scotland and Burgundy. St. Benedict of Nursia established the roots of a reformed monasticism. And Charles Martel drove the Muslim Saracens *out of* Spain once again—indeed, out of Europe for centuries to come. But nothing very good ever seemed to last long in these *Mad Max*–like conditions: violence, rapine, pillage, and famine were always hiding just around the corner. Time and time again, the Church fell into a lax, anarchic condition and teetered on the verge of outright collapse. "For more than three-score years," wrote St. Boniface, in a 742 letter to Pope Zachary,

> all ecclesiastical order and discipline has been set at naught and trodden underfoot; for more than eighty years, the Franks have not held a synod or had an archbishop, nor have the laws of the Church been enforced anywhere in all that time. The episcopal sees are for the most part in the hands of avaricious laymen or of dissolute ecclesiastics, who hold them as temporary possessions. No wickedness is a bar to the priesthood or the episcopacy.[15]

Boniface labored to bring these churches at the back edge of civilization into closer union with the papacy again, assisted by Charles Martel's two grandsons, Carloman and Carolus.

A few years later, when Carolus (Charles in Latin) succeeded to the kingship of the Franks, he marched to Rome and freed the Holy City from the Arian Lombards still oppressing it. Then, for the next thirty years, he fought to extend his own rule—in partnership with that of the pope—over all the barbarians of the West.

---

[15] Thomas Bokenkotter, *A Concise History of the Catholic Church* (New York: Image Books, 1977), 98.

Finally, having earned the name Charles the Great (Charlemagne in French), he virtually reconstituted the old political unity of the Western Roman Empire, leaving some to wonder if he hadn't, in the process, effectively made himself the first Western Caesar in three hundred years. Even so, Charlemagne was as surprised as anyone when, on Christmas Day in the year 800, Pope Leo III—in response, it would seem, to a sudden inspiration—set a crown on Charles's head. The spontaneous ceremony sent a thrill through the large congregation assembled for Mass, causing them to cry out, "Hail, Charles the Augustus, crowned of God, the great pacifier and emperor of the Romans!"

However it happened, it was a glorious moment. For the first time in centuries, Europeans had a true champion again: Catholic in his faith, like the great Christian emperors of antiquity, brave and resolute in battle, a founder of schools and patron of scholars, eager to bring order where there had been only chaos. To be honest, the pope's act had more of hope in it than of substance. An emperor with no Roman legions, no Roman treasury or Roman courts, no Senate, no imperial machinery of any kind, Charlemagne ruled over men's imaginations more anything else—and imagination is where the dream of civilization has always begun, as Pope Leo must have known.

In this way, the pope's act is rather akin to another of those memorable apocalypse movies: 1997's *The Postman*. In it, as some will remember, a nameless drifter, wandering the wastelands of a collapsed United States, rallies the hopes of fellow survivors using nothing more than a dead postman's uniform and a sack of undelivered mail.

Charlemagne, too, by evoking an emperor even when no empire existed, worked on humanity's hopes like the mailbag in the movie—a memory of the world that once was, representing the ghost of a chance that law and order might really have been reinstated someplace, a hope against hope. For a few splendid years, that hope was enough.

While Charlemagne lived, the dream lived. Conditions began to improve everywhere, in both civic and ecclesiastical matters. Had things gone well, the Western Roman Empire might have revived — might even have outlived the Eastern Roman Empire or reunited with it and survived to this day. But when Charlemagne died and left his realm to unworthy heirs (Louis the Pious and his four fractious sons) the whole undertaking disintegrated as quickly as it had arisen, taking the Western Church down with it — to a degree few of us today can even imagine.

The despair, in fact, that came from having seen a light at the end of the tunnel and then slowly realizing it was only a mirage made things worse. Even many good people threw up their hands and surrendered themselves to the madness. Drunkenness was everywhere, fields went unplowed, and famine returned. Strange, apocalyptic cults arose, tempting the people to horrifying superstitions. The process was accelerated by new waves of barbarian invasion. Emboldened by the fall of the Carolingians, the pagan Magyars overran Christian Hungary; Viking pirates raided the northern coasts at will, plundering churches and destroying the flowering Irish monasteries. To the south, Islam grew stronger and stronger, conquering Sicily and Crete and even establishing a foothold in lower Italy. What little government existed in Western Europe was now undertaken by local bosses, petty chieftains coarsened and made cruel by the long conflict with savages.

Pretty quickly, these bosses took control of the only thing left worth stealing — the Catholic Church. They could not simply have liquidated Church wealth at this point and deposited it all in their own coffers: what was left of a faithful laity would not have stood for it. So they did the next best thing—they put their own handpicked men into practically every office of the Church. Political functionaries were made priests; laymen were made bishops and installed into vital episcopal sees. Huge monastic estates were signed over to freebooters in miters. *Simony*—named for wicked Simon Magus from the Acts of the Apostles, who offered money to the apostles to gain the gifts of the Spirit (for which he had a lucrative use outside the Church [Acts 8:9ff.])—became the besetting sin of the age.

The bosses—now doing business under the titles of prince and baron—began taking money from men who wanted to be ordained: men, in other words, willing to be priests for a price. "If they could give guarantees to their sovereign of their fidelity to his dynasty and to his politics," writes Father Laux in his *Church History*,

> that was considered more important than if they could interpret Scripture, preach a sermon, or write a learned treatise. Usually, to be successful, the aspirant to office had to be endorsed by some powerful courtier. But the courtiers did not give their patronage free of charge; they sold it to the highest bidder. Most of the bishops, therefore, bought their office, and in their turn sold the dignities of a secondary order; and the lower clergy, to reimburse themselves, sold the sacraments and the sacramentals.[16]

There must have been good men among the clergy during these dark days, trying to rise above it all, but if so, they've

---

[16] Fr. John Laux, *Church History* (Charlotte, NC: TAN Books, 2012), 264.

left precious little mark on the records. In all likelihood, not even all the bosses were true scoundrels. Some probably meant well, but they all believed, from their own crude, this-worldly perspective, that times like these called for soldiers, not saints, in the seats of authority. Not too surprisingly then, the morals of both clergy and religious began to resemble those of soldiers. As historian Philip Hughes puts it, with bishops "more baron than Father-in-God, and priests as rude as the illiterate serfs to whom they ministered, such a refinement of ecclesiastical discipline as the mystic celibacy was exposed to altogether unheard-of losses."

Perhaps the most common of these immoralities was the village priest shacked up with a common-law wife. Yes, celibacy was still mandatory, so priests who married committed sin in doing so. But the marriage that resulted from such a sin was still held to be valid—and things had sunk so low that his congregants weren't really all that scandalized. The pastor often brought his new wife to live at the rectory with him.

Trouble was, these illicit marriages, by their very nature, seldom took place in public; the nuptials, in other words, left no witnesses. So if, as was often the case, no real ceremony ever occurred—if, in other words, the woman involved had married her clergyman "without benefit of clergy"—no one knew the difference. The fine shade of distinction between a "pastor living in the usual illicit marriage" and "the pastor living in sin with his mistress—on church property!" became too academic to pursue; and the people, again, had gotten to where they didn't really care.

To compound matters even further, the sons of such unions often became priests themselves and took over their fathers' benefices (that is, the church properties associated with their office and from which they drew their pay in the form of rents).

A clerical caste began to form; and there were even efforts to make the great bishoprics hereditary, like a crown of royalty.

It was inevitable under conditions like these that the papacy, too, would fall into the hands of venal men—and boy, did it ever! With Charlemagne gone, the pope's office was up for grabs as much as any, and the bosses conspired together to take it in hand, like the Corleone family gaining the "friendship" of a city alderman. Secular princes elected popes, deposed them at their own discretion, sometimes installed the deposed man a second time, and even murdered several to get them out of the way.

Before offering these sad puppets too much of our sympathy, it's best to know that many of them were very happy to play along with this game, and that several of them were as bad as or worse than their masters.

Let us take a few pages now to hit, for the purposes of this chronicle of bad shepherds, a few of the low points.

When the last of Charlemagne's grandsons died, there was a bit of a free-for-all over who should inherit what remained of Grandfather's revived Roman Empire (that reduced portion, mainly German, known in later years as the *Holy Roman Empire*). Pope Formosus (elected in 891) reluctantly crowned Lambert Duke of Spoleto but much preferred his own patron, the East Frankish king Arnulf. Later, Formosus secretly persuaded Arnulf to march on Rome, liberate the city from Lambert, and then be crowned emperor at his hands in Lambert's stead. Before the matter played itself out fully, however, Formosus died (perhaps by poisoning) and was replaced by Boniface VI. Boniface—a man who had already been defrocked twice, as a subdeacon and then as a priest—was made pope by a pro-Arnulf Roman mob. The unworthiness of Boniface did not matter long, because he, too, under mysterious circumstances after a pontificate of just fifteen days, was soon dead. He was succeeded by Stephen VII, himself the son of an unworthy priest, now a bishop ordained by Formosus—but rabidly pro-Lambert. And with Stephen's 896 election as pope, Rome was made safe for the Dukes of Spoleto.

Afterward, Pope Stephen was prevailed upon by his puppeteers to perform one of the weirdest, most grisly acts of religious history: the trial and condemnation, *post-mortem*, of his predecessor Formosus. The rage of the still quasi-civilized Spoleto barons was so fierce that they demanded that the pope convene a whole synod for this purpose and arranged that Formosus himself—stone dead for nine months, mind you—should appear in the docket in person. The ex-pope's corpse, still wearing the papal vestments in which it was buried, was disinterred and propped up on a papal throne in the judgment hall. A junior deacon was named his court-appointed defender, and this man stood by his client throughout the proceedings, ready to answer the charges against Formosus should the accused elect to exercise (as many expected) his right to remain silent. The verdict, of course, was a foregone conclusion. Formosus was found guilty of a number of canonical irregularities and other accusations, many of them true. But his real crime, as everyone knew, had been to put himself on the wrong side of the victorious party in a nasty dust-up over the right to Charlemagne's throne.

At the sentencing, all the acts of Pope Formosus were annulled (including all his ordinations—which should have rendered Stephen himself a layman but somehow didn't), and all his measures were rescinded.

To symbolize this, Pope Stephen ordered the three fingers that the dead pope had used to confer his ordinations to be severed from his right hand and burned. The rest of the body was stripped, handed over to a jeering rabble, and dragged through

the streets before being dumped, finally, into the Tiber. Fortu-
nately, it was fished out by a pious monk and reburied with full
honors about a year later, once Stephen had died—strangled in
a prison cell—during additional intrigues.

In the bad-shepherd annals of infamy, all this became known
as the *Synodus Horrenda*, or the Cadaver Synod. About the best
we can say is that it was ginned up at the demand of Lambert and
his cronies rather than by Stephen himself, but if the pope had
any objections to the obscene spectacle, he kept them to himself.

Fifty years later, the Dukes of Spoleto managed a real coup:
they got one of their sons elected both pope and emperor *at the
same time*, theoretically creating the most powerful man who had
ever lived, sovereign over both the spiritual *and* temporal goods
of Christendom. Not surprisingly, young Octavian—eighteen
years old when he first sat on the Chair of Peter—made a hash
of both jobs.

His father, Alberic, ordered his ascent to the papacy. The
Western emperors had been choosing popes for years now, virtually
unchallenged, and now Alberic made his nobles swear to support,
when the time came, his own son for the job. When Alberic
died before the bishopric of Rome came open, young Octavian
became emperor first, then cardinal-deacon of Santa Maria for a
few months, and finally Pope John XII (only the third instance
in history of a new pontiff taking a regnal name upon elevation
to the chair rather than using his own).

Charity suggests that we chalk it all up to his youth. Like
a rock star shooting for an early grave, he got too much fame
and fortune too fast. For John XII did not let his spiritual duties
interfere with his enjoyment of the usual imperial perquisites.
He laughed and had a good time. He spent most of his hours
gambling and whoring. He did enjoy a good hunt, and hawking

and gaming, and even led troops in war from time to time, which he also seemed to enjoy. He was not stingy. John gave Church lands away to his girlfriends in much the same way Elvis gave Cadillacs.

Even so, from time to time, John did make some attempt to look like a pope — early in his pontificate, at any rate. In 958, he granted special privileges to St. Benedict's old abbey, on the condition that the priests and monks there should, "every day, recite, for the good of our soul and that of our successors, a hundred *Kyrie eleisons* and a hundred *Christe eleisons*, and that thrice each week the priests should offer the Holy Mass to Almighty God for the absolution of our soul and those of our successors." Not long after that, he received a visit from St. Dunstan, whom he made archbishop of Canterbury with his own hands. Still, this kind of stuff certainly was not John's forte, and he seemed, to many, rather bored with the whole thing.

When, a couple of years in, two of his rivals for the empire made alarming gains, John (or rather, Octavian, as he still signed his name on secular documents) took quick, decisive action. He begged the vigorous King Otto of Saxony to come and take his place as emperor. Otto was a good man, but he shared the idea, common by this time, that popes were primarily civil servants hired to run the empire's "Department of Religious Affairs." He agreed to assume the emperor's crown and even agreed to let John keep his other job, though word of his unfitness was well out by this time. After he was crowned, Otto insisted that John/Octavian reform his dissolute lifestyle and pledge obedience to him and to all future Holy Roman emperors. John agreed, but (as events will demonstrate) with his fingers metaphorically crossed behind his back. Otto took immediately to the battlefield to fend off the two rivals. John's cowardly act had tremendous historical consequences, as it turned out; for it put the empire into the hands of the German Franks for the next 844 years.

Nevertheless, the twenty-four-year-old pope regretted his act as soon as Otto was gone. Worried, perhaps, that the new emperor might force him to make good on his pledge of reform, he took steps to limit Otto's power. He even encouraged the Byzantine emperor to reassert his claims over the West now that it was slowly becoming stable enough again to be worth his while. Unfortunately for John, Otto intercepted the treacherous letters. The emperor finished his military business quickly—then marched his army directly back to Rome.

Learning of Otto's approach, Pope John planned initially to hole up in his castle; but he quickly realized the futility of it and fled instead, hauling away as much of the papal treasury as his entourage could carry. When the emperor arrived and found the pope gone, he summoned a synod to be held at St. Peter's in Rome (the old St. Peter's, the one that was demolished in 1505 to make room for today's basilica) for the purpose of deposing John, not only for his recent misconduct but for gross immorality as well. John was ordered by letter to appear. He refused, of course, writing the following response instead, in very poor Latin: "To all the bishops—We hear that you wish to make another pope. If you do, I excommunicate you by almighty God and you have no power to ordain no one or celebrate Mass." The fifty German and Italian bishops went ahead anyway, commencing a trial that interviewed dozens of witnesses.

Some commentators have wondered how fair John's trial really was, given the standards of the day and the political forces involved (and it is true that the records of the trial were mostly preserved by partisans of the emperor). Still, the many independent accounts of John's conduct, even from parties hostile to the German emperors, leave us little reason to doubt that this rock-star pope—this really bad shepherd—had given Otto's prosecutors a wealth of material to work with.

His constant acts of simony were, perhaps, par for the course for a tenth-century cleric. Benedict, his successor as cardinal-deacon of Rome, testified that John had ordained dozens of bishops at a price, including a ten-year-old boy. This bishop of Narni had been personally present, he said, when John ordained a wealthy horse trader for money while still inside the stable where the offer was made. His other enormities must have been more shocking at the time, though the rumors had always been rampant.

House servants testified that the pope practically made the sacred palace into a brothel. They named names: Anna, the widow of Count Rainier, Stephana (who had been his father's mistress!), even his own niece. When he wasn't fornicating, John spent his time shooting dice, fighting duels, drinking heavily—even, with a wink in his eye, raising a glass to the devil on regular occasions. While placing his bets, he invoked the aid of Jupiter, Venus, and other pagan gods. When his confessor happened to witness one of his indiscretions, John had his eyes poked out. The wounds grew infected, and the priest died. When another cleric in the palace thought to partake in the fun himself, taking one of the pope's cast-offs into his own bed, John had him castrated. Another romantic rival had his house burned down. Priests who assisted him at Mass said that the pope almost never took the Sacrament and avoided making the Sign of the Cross. The emperor himself testified against his predecessor.

At the end of the trial, the synod fathers concluded that the successor of Peter had conducted himself more like Nero, the murderer of Peter. With Otto's consent, they declared him deposed on December 4, 963, and ordered court officers to find him and take him, dead or alive. They replaced John with a new pope, Leo VIII, who was no real prize himself—in fact, John had previously sent him to Otto with a pack of lies about the progress of the young pope's moral reformation. Nevertheless, Leo (a layman to this point!) was, within the space of a single day, ordained a lector, an acolyte, a subdeacon, a deacon, a priest, a bishop, and finally, the pope. Then the council disbanded and left town. The emperor had already been called away to battle once more, against those rivals of John who had now become the rivals of Otto.

Ex-Pope John managed one more wave of outrages before going to his reward. In Otto's absence, he stirred up his remaining sympathizers in Rome, offering them large bribes (out of stolen Church funds, naturally) to kick Leo out. Several Roman nobles took the bait, causing the new pope to flee to the protection of the emperor's army. This allowed John to return to Rome briefly and stage a council of his own, declaring Leo's election invalid (which was at least partially true, since his election proceedings had included several important irregularities).

John stayed just long enough to take vengeance on many of those who testified against him—a cardinal had his hands cut off, a city official lost his nose and ears, Bishop Otgar of Speyer was scourged—before fleeing, once more, at the reported approach of Otto. Not long after this, Octavian, son of Alberic, once both emperor and pope, died in a private house on the outskirts of the city. Though the reports are somewhat confused and rhetorical (one version says the devil himself came and took him), the most likely version has him killed by an outraged husband while engaged in the act of adultery. So much for the rock-star pope.

Finally, we come to Benedict IX, who has the strange distinction of having served as pope *three separate times* (1032–1044, 1045, 1047–1048). Another useless wastrel elevated by his father to the Fisherman's see at a ridiculously young age (perhaps as young as twelve!), this bad shepherd gave John XII a genuine run for his money in the domain of debauchery. Benedict was the nephew of his two immediate predecessors (which ought to give you some idea of how the office was regarded during the Age of Iron) but while both—Benedict VIII and John XIX—had been halfway decent considering the times, the new Benedict really was little more than a party animal wearing the papal tiara. The less said, perhaps, the better when it comes to the details at this point. The outline is suggested by the following memorable sentence from Catholic writer Mike Aquilina: "Some historians believe that he was mostly homosexual, although not exclusively, to judge by the complaints made by aristocratic husbands in Rome."[17]

Benedict's real achievement, as we have already mentioned, is the feat of having been pope three times; no one else has managed it even twice. His first pontificate ended abruptly when an angry mob, perhaps stirred up by his family's political enemies, attempted to kill him inside his own church. This wicked pope fled into the night, leaving pro- and anti-Benedict factions to brawl in the streets of Rome for half a year. Those who opposed him needed a quick substitute to thwart Benedict's return, and so they sold the papacy to another worthless cleric, Bishop John of Sabina, whom they declared to be Pope Sylvester III. Never properly installed, Sylvester is remembered today (if at all) as an antipope. Benedict returned, however, at the head of a private

---

[17] Mike Aquilina, *Good Pope, Bad Pope; Their Lives, Our Lessons* (Cincinnati: Servant Books, 2013), 82.

army, and kicked "Sylvester" out—the beginning of his second pontificate.

Less than a year later, however, Benedict became infatuated with his cousin and decided to have her as his wife. Perhaps it was his idea of "settling down" and ceasing to sow wild oats. At any rate, the notion of a married pope was a bridge too far even in the eleventh century. No pope had ever resigned before, but it *was* theoretically possible—and soon Benedict's people were pressuring him to do just that. Benedict wasn't willing to leave the matter to chance, though: he picked his own successor. To avoid as much further scandal as possible, he cleverly selected a pious but rather thick fellow with a clean record, the archpriest John Gratian. He still, however, wouldn't just *give* the prize away: Benedict offered to resign and make John pope ... *upon receipt of one thousand pounds of gold.* John likely agreed to the transaction solely for the good of the Church, chiefly to get Benedict quickly off the property; he may even have raised the money by subscription. Even so, "an event now occurred which has no parallel in the history of the Church: Benedict abdicated in favor of the Archpriest John Gratian for a good round sum of money. The highest office in Christendom had been bought and sold. Simon Magus had achieved his greatest triumph."[18]

Now, like a renaissance farce, everything blew up at once to tragicomic effect. Benedict's cousin spurned him, leaving the ex-pope to simmer volcanically at the altar. The jilted bridegroom concluded abruptly that the new pontiff (who had taken a reformer's name, Gregory) was tainted with simony—perfectly true—and thus not fit to serve. So Benedict wanted his old job back. Finally, so-called Sylvester III popped back up, injecting

---

[18] Laux, *Church History*, 272.

his dubious claims into the mix. Thus, in the autumn of 1046, there came to be three popes in Rome at once, each claiming to be the one and only true successor of poor old St. Peter: Gregory VI at the Vatican, Benedict holed up in the Lateran Palace, and Sylvester biding his time at the Church of St. Mary Major. At that point, most of the Roman laity came to their senses, prayed a pox upon all these fools and knaves, and wrote away to obtain, once more, the intervention of the Holy Roman emperor.

Make no mistake: interference in Church government on the part of secular authorities is a very bad thing—though the story had gotten too old to excite much protest by this stage of history. And it's awfully hard to blame those who called for it, considering the spectacle on view here. But whether for good or for ill, the emperor did send his son Henry III, king of Germany, down to Rome to knock a little sense into the situation.

Sometime after his arrival (backed up by troops, of course), Henry emerged from a smoke-filled room with the final settlement. The well-meaning Gregory would resign voluntarily for the sake of peace; in fact, he immediately pronounced sentence upon himself: "I, Gregory, bishop, servant of the servants of God, because of the simony which, by the cunning of the devil, entered into my election, decide that I must be deposed from the Roman bishopric."

Sylvester was declared (correctly) never to have been pope at all; he was ordered to a monastery so that he might finish his days at prayer and trouble the Church no more.

Benedict IX, the original claimant and the last pope standing, was deposed as well for having twice abdicated of his own free will, both times for cash. It had been a full day's work for King Henry, no doubt about it. He had deposed three Roman pontiffs since breakfast. And now, as the sun went down behind the Seven Hills, Rome had no pope at all.

Still, that's only—what, one, two actual papacies for Benedict? He had made claims to a third, to be sure, but never took office. Well, there is, believe it or not, an absurd postscript. Before leaving town, Henry offered the bishops a new candidate, an unusually religious man this time, a German bishop named Suidger, whom they soon installed as Pope Clement II. Alas, Clement sickened and died within a year—at which point, believe it or not, *Benedict IX reappeared*, spreading bribes around so thickly that he actually did manage to break the all-time world record: yes, his third and final papacy. Henry was so incensed when he got the news, he threatened to march on Rome with an overwhelming force and hang every man jack involved. This finally did the trick, and Benedict left town for the last time, thank God. "At last the Temple had been cleared of the buyers and sellers, of those who had made it a den of thieves and a reproach among the nations."[19]

Many writers have noted that the reign(s) of Benedict IX may have been a blessing in disguise. As Mike Aquilina continues, "Sometimes absolute rottenness can be a great mercy. A mildly venal pope would have been business as usual; the dysfunction in the curia could have festered for generations more. But Benedict, by being the worst possible pope, gave the reformers the kick they needed."

One of these reformers truly did end up being the silver-lining under Benedict's cloud. The hapless Pope Gregory VI had a friend named Hildebrand, a fiery young monk of St. Mary on the Aventine, and Hildebrand ended up becoming one of the greatest reforming popes of all time. He attacked all the abuses he had seen during his friend's ill-starred pontificate—even the ones committed by Gregory himself. He strove to enforce

19 Ibid., 264.

vigorously the rule of celibacy for the first time in centuries. He summoned a council to confront simony and excommunicated those who resisted. He also excommunicated the Holy Roman emperor, Henry IV, no fewer than three times in a fight to release papal authority from under the thumb of secular princes. Though he did not complete the job himself—somehow your recently scrubbed kitchen floor always gets dirty again—things were never the same after Hildebrand. And, significantly, he chose *Gregory VII* as his own regnal name, perhaps to show that even a well-meaning lunkhead like his sponsor, not without sins of his own to repent, might just merit the E for effort.

Chapter 3

Resisters of Reform:
Clerical Collapse in the Disastrous
Fourteenth Century

Yes, the Church overcame the Age of Iron, survived its bad shepherds, and revived. The reforms begun by Hildebrand and other monks of Cluny ushered in an unparalleled age of reform; and the reforms worked miracles. When they were complete, the new Ages of Faith had been born, and devils like John XII and Stephen VII were banished to the outer darkness. But what of the laity during the Dark Ages? Haven't we maintained that the laity often thrives during times when the clergy are at their worst? Can that really have been true under the semibarbarous conditions we just reviewed?

It *must* have been true — and here's why. Though literacy was rare in those days and the people who *were* literate were often clerics writing about clerical heroes; and though records, in such circumstances, are kept only about exceptional people; we can deduce the presence of many unnamed heroes as well, just from the facts of the case. The Catholic laity of the West were not, for the most part, men and women of a totally different stock from that of the Lombards or the Goths they resisted; ethnically, the original Greco-Roman population was a minority by this time.

No, by this point, the people who resisted the barbarians had lately been barbarians themselves. So what they hated and what they shed their blood to exorcise, was *the way of the barbarians*—which, as we have seen, was semipagan Arianism and the like. What the ordinary Christian people held to—despite their bad shepherds and at so great a price—was traditional, Christ-honoring Christianity (as expressed in the Nicene definitions).

No Ernie Pyle has immortalized his story, but orthodoxy's "G.I. Joe"—the regular Western layman—*must* have existed during the Dark Ages, or there would have been nothing left to reform when Gregory VII came along. There are other evidences as well. The men and women who responded to the calls of Columba, of Benedict, of Boniface, and of other monastics must, after all, have come originally from the *ranks of a pious laity*. But the willingness of the West as a whole to resist rule by defective forms of Christ-evoking religion really is the greatest proof that the laity of the Dark Ages was anything but a flock of sheep frightened by their bad shepherds.

In the Ages of Faith, the lay heroes step fully into the light. Many, if not most, of the greatest figures of the period are, in fact, Catholic laypeople, exhibiting the Lordship of Christ over the whole realm of human endeavor: Chaucer, Dante, Giotto, Petrarch, Marco Polo, St. Louis IX, and Richard the Lionheart. "The Church had effected a complete transformation and revival of the races of Western Europe."[20] From this point, Christendom actually became a reality: it was "the period during which our people, our culture were most themselves, when the effect of the religion which made us was wholly mature, complete, and

---

[20] J. P. Kirsch, "The Reformation," *Catholic Encyclopedia* (New York: Robert Appleton, 1911).

victorious."[21] The popes had become arbiters of a continent-wide peace; the papacy had finally achieved a working equilibrium with the secular powers; and the population began to be healed, fed, inspired, and educated by the great monasteries of Europe. This was the age of Magna Carta, of the beginnings of self-government, the period when universities were invented and even the poor were welcome to attend.

But sadly, it isn't the purpose of this book to depict those wonderful days when most things went right. We're here right now to be reminded that men, including bishops and popes, are, after all, not gods—and that we are not to expect heaven on earth. We must therefore reluctantly get back to the business at hand and watch a little longer as the glories of the High Middle Ages crumble away under the corrosion of human sin and folly. Happily, we have that famous saying of Chesterton to steel us here at the halfway point: "Yes, Christendom has had a series of revolutions and in each one of them Christianity has died. Christianity has died many times and risen again; for it had a God who knew the way out of the grave."

Three major forces brought about the dissolution of Catholic civilization as the Middle Ages grew old. For each of the three, history has supplied us with a goat—a Catholic leader who fiddled while Rome burned or, worse, actively resisted the nearly universal cry for *reformatio in capite et in membris* (reform in the head and in the members). Bad shepherds, in fact, were the *chief obstacle to reform* in those days; most of the serious reform efforts were commenced by laypeople, secular leaders, and, sometimes, religious monks and sisters. Many of the worst abuses, in fact,

---

[21] Hilaire Belloc, *The Crisis of Civilization* (Charlotte, NC: TAN Books, 1992), 92.

were *created by the clergy*; and even those that were not, created selfish advantages for clergymen that a large coalition of them did not intend to lose. All the while, rage against these abuses grew ever more intense. The catastrophe did finally take place — that vast, chaotic flood of a thousand mutually exclusive "reforms" at once, which is usually called the Protestant Reformation.

Worldliness was the chief sin going in; eyes off the prize once again, eyes turned instead to politics, money, privilege, and territorialism. The higher clergy, in particular, seem to have believed that, with everyone now safely baptized, their job as shepherds was pretty much completed. The task was *administrative* going forward, mainly concerned with the settling of disputes among Christian men — the episcopate had become, in other words, little more than a clutch of politicians. As a result, their lifestyles began to resemble those of shady politicians. The papal Curia lived in such a way as to be wholly indistinguishable from the secular nobles of their day, to whom they were usually related by blood. In the controversies of the day, they sided with the pope or with one of his enemies based on which way the wind was blowing. The money required to maintain their princely habits was gained by riding on the backs of a heavily taxed lower clergy and finding clever ways to skim the rents on Church property. Obviously, mere spoilsmen like these were ill prepared, character-wise, to pilot Peter's barque through the stormy seas ahead.

Ordinarily, this clerical professionalism would have been overcome in the presence of a crisis. The bad shepherds might have risen to the occasion, as the deeply divided American people and their leaders overcame the lethargy of the 1930s immediately after Pearl Harbor. But the turn of the fourteenth century — the 1300s — brought virtually unprecedented disaster: not one enormous existential crisis with which to grapple but *three at once.* The Church, with her power of rebirth and renewal, would have taken one crisis in her stride and might even have survived two at once, like white blood cells fighting off multiple infections. Along with sinners, there were, after all, great people on the job—some of the greatest, in fact: Catherine of Siena, Vincent Ferrer, Julian of Norwich, Thomas à Kempis, and Bridget of Sweden. But three cataclysms at once proved too much even for these. Overwhelmed, many of the clergy seemed almost to have surrendered, even ramping up their own abuses in the spirit of "every man for himself."

The first of these fourteenth-century tragedies was the *Avignon papacy and the Great Western Schism* that followed. Together, these destroyed for many Christians the very concept of a single, universal Church, directly opening the door to the later privatization—we almost might say *atomization*—of religious belief in the centuries ahead.

Here's how it happened. The city of Rome was a riot in the early 1300s—one long series of riots, rather, between political and ecclesiastical factions. Papal elections began to be tainted by threats of violence, and one pope was held prisoner for a while and was pressured to resign.

The dangers of the Age of Iron were over; the Church had not become subservient, as she threatened to do at that time, to the German emperors and their Italian allies. Now the balance was tipping in another direction as *the French monarchy* attempted to achieve European hegemony. Having the popes in their pockets would mean a rubber stamp on all their future plans, for, as we previously noted, the papacy acted as a kind of UN Security Council during the Middle Ages and often, by threats of interdict and excommunication, stopped what it deemed unjust aggression. So when Pope Clement V—a candidate favored by the French—was elected in 1309, King Philip IV offered to bring him to France, where he could be crowned "in safety." Clement agreed—and never left French territory again. He ultimately moved the whole papal court to the city of Avignon in Provence—moved, in other words, the papacy itself—and there it remained for nearly seventy years. Avignon technically belonged to vassals of the pope, but everyone knew it was totally dominated by France and by French culture. All seven of the popes during this era were Frenchmen, as were 111 of 134 new cardinals. Historians ever since have referred to this period as "the Babylonian Captivity of the Papacy."

Clement wasn't really one of the bad shepherds; he was no more or less conniving and pecuniary than any other average fourteenth-century churchman. But the move itself was a calamity.

So long as the popes reigned from Rome, they stood on the shoulders of Peter—almost literally (the Fisherman's bones are buried under St. Peter's). The popes symbolized centrality, universality, and impartiality for every European citizen, just as the Roman Empire had once done. The pope *out of Rome*, on the other hand, a mere adornment of one particular European power and employed for its own ends, began to seem ... dispensable.

And the Holy City, emptied of Peter's presence for the first time since the apostolic era, grew weeded and stagnant. The population declined, and many of its churches and other monuments deteriorated. The whole situation was almost a visible symbol of *Christianity with the steering wheel off*—a pretty good description for the centuries ahead, even after the popes returned.

Pope Urban V tried to return in 1367. Sixth of the Avignon popes, Urban is actually one of the good guys in our story; he was a Benedictine monk who continued to follow Benedict's rule, living simply and frugally even as pope. He made the other clerics at Avignon look bad, and they resented it deeply. His attempt to reestablish the papacy in its natural home failed, however, due, once again, to political chaos on the Tiber. He was forced to return to Avignon (and thus to French custody) within three years. Finally, Gregory XI, Urban's successor, accomplished the miracle in 1377, through the intercession, support, and, well, nagging of St. Catherine of Siena. The captivity was over, but the worst was yet to come.

Gregory died in Rome, so the new pontiff would be elected in Rome. The French monarchy wanted another Frenchman, of course, and had packed the College of Cardinals with Frenchmen with just this thought in mind. The people of Rome however, were skewed heavily pro-Italian and pro-German, and they were determined to make themselves heard. In fact, as the cardinals marched to the conclave, they were heckled in the street: "Give us a Roman pope, or we will make your heads redder than your hats!"

Lest this advice should be misunderstood or neglected, during the proceedings, the Romans also stacked firewood — loudly — in the chamber directly below the room where the choice was being made. Knowing this fact goes a long way toward explaining the quick selection of Bartolomeo Prignano, born in Itri, just down the coast from the Holy City.

He chose the name Urban VI, but the new pope was nothing whatsoever like his immediate predecessor. If there was ever a time in Church history that called for a peacemaker, a unifier, someone to mediate mutual concessions and pour oil on the troubled waters, this was it. And yet Urban VI deliberately did just exactly and precisely the opposite.

As soon as the coronation ended, he went on a crusade of reform against the French cardinals and Curia. He attacked gifts and gratuities, luxury and immorality, their multiple bishoprics, and other acts of simony (so far, so good), but strangely, all were subjects in which Urban himself had shown little or no interest heretofore.

What Urban *had* been doing all his life was growing more and more irate against French domination of the Church. As the first pope after Avignon, he was a fiasco. It was like electing Jefferson Davis to the presidency of the United States immediately after General Grant. Urban VI deliberately plunged the Church into turmoil at the worst possible moment, fully displaying the madness of partisanship to which the political clergy of this era had become captive.

The men who elected him quickly took themselves out of his reach. Convening again at Anagni, they declared Peter's chair empty (*sede vacante*) because of the duress under which Urban had been elected. Then they chose and appointed another "pope"—surprise, a Frenchman!—and called him Clement VII. After that, they packed Clement off to Avignon, where they all looked forward to resuming business as usual.

When Urban heard about it, he dismissed every single French cardinal in the Church and replaced them all with Italians. Clement got word of this and promptly identified Urban as the Antichrist and immediately excommunicated him. This was the beginning of the Great Western Schism ... a dumbfounding breach that lasted thirty-nine years.

There had, of course, been multiple claimants to the papal throne before this, as we saw so vividly in the previous chapter. Here was the difference this time: both Urban VI at Rome and the new Clement VII in France (who quickly set up a complete papal court there, founding a second line of Avignon popes) had been elected *by the same group of men*, not by the leaders of competing factions.

So which pope was pope?

Europe immediately started choosing sides. The deliberations were careful, of course: sober, prayerful, and made by men with rock-solid credentials. But in the end, everyone voted just as the rudest peasant expected they would, having seen the result coming a mile off. The Germans, most of the Italians, and their allies, the English, the Poles, and the Hungarians, all determined that Urban was still the true pope. The French, along with their allies, the Burgundians, the Cypriots, and the Scots, all decided Clement was clearly the genuine article. To the layman—still praying for the pope at every Mass, whoever that might happen to be—it was all deeply, deeply upsetting.

The great Italian humanist Coluccio Salutati, who attended the conclave that chose Clement, had seen through the whole thing from the start: "Who does not see," he asked the French cardinals, "that you seek not the true pope, but opt solely for a Gallic pontiff?" St. Catherine cut to the chase as well: "devils in human form" was her description of the men who would have carried the papacy to France once more.

And, in fact, later scholars and canonists did finally prove that the so-called Clement had been the antipope at this point, with Urban, for all his faults, the actual successor of Peter. But, as far as public perception went, the damage by these bad shepherds was done, and the grotesque affair seemed, for many, to bring the whole concept of apostolic succession into question, setting the stage for the Protestants to come.

Indeed, the thing may even have driven Urban himself mad. First, Louis of Anjou, heir apparent to the French throne, essentially put a bounty on the pope's head. He carved out a new kingdom from French-held papal territories and offered it to any nobleman who could extract Urban from Castel Sant'Angelo and bring him to Paris to receive "justice." The castle was besieged, and the pope fled to Naples. Later, as he sought to recruit allies there, Urban was arrested and imprisoned. He ranted, raged, and denounced for six months, performing solemn acts of excommunication in his cell all day long.

When he was finally rescued by the Doge of Genoa, the men who released him were shocked at his wild, unstable manner, at which point a group of his own cardinals tried to declare him mentally unfit—which Urban, of course, looked on as just another attempt remove him from the Chair. He had the "conspirators" arrested and tortured to death, a crime "unheard of through the centuries," according to the historian Antonini. An old story, in fact (which may or may not be true), insists that Urban personally berated the jailers when the screams he heard issuing from the torture chamber did not seem anguished enough.

By the time the schism was healed, both Urban and Clement had been dead for decades. When the Council of Constance finally resolved the tragic farce in 1414 by electing Martin V (clearing away at least three other contenders!) there was one pope in Rome again, accepted at last by all of Christendom—but the prestige of the papacy was never the same. The chickens had come home to roost after a century of very bad shepherds: popes and bishops who thought of themselves primarily as princes.

The second of these fourteenth-century disasters—fully simultaneous with Avignon and the Great Schism—was the arrival of the *Black Death* in Christendom—perhaps the most destructive pandemic in world history, which killed, by very reliable estimates, about half the population of Europe. In some areas the death toll may have been as high as 80 percent.

It was a visitation upon a scale so enormous as to strike a blow at medieval society which might have dissolved it—and nearly did dissolve it.... In some places towns and villages sank never to rise again.... You may trace its effects even today in the half-finished buildings which were stopped dead and their completion never undertaken.[22]

It's no wonder many Catholics believed that Pestilence, the first of St. John's Four Horsemen, had made his prophesied appearance (see Rev. 6).

One of the cruelest ironies about the Black Death is the way it contributed so heavily to the deterioration of the clergy. In what way? Imagine the workload for a priest: confessions, last rites, comfort to survivors, and Christian burial (when possible) from sunup to sundown for weeks, months, years on end. And though science did not yet know what caused the Black Death, everyone knew very well by common sense alone that whoever spent time around the plague usually died from it sooner or later. So the clergy who took the sacraments into the plague zones were spiritually akin to the firemen who ran *toward* the Twin Towers on 9/11 while everyone else was running away. The faithful bishop, the loyal priest, the dutiful deacon all ministered as long as they could, and then died. The cowards and deserters fled and survived—to become practically the whole clergy in the postplague years. No wonder the fifteenth century was such a dumpster fire.

As a direct result of this factor, the Faith itself got lost somewhere along the way—or adulterated, at any rate, by a nasty tincture of superstition. The plague shut down churches and monasteries, all the places where the real Christian Faith was

---

[22] Belloc, *The Crisis of Civilization*, 89.

meant to be taught (and had been for a long time, despite individual lapses).

Many of the clergy ordained to replace the fallen became "Mass priests"— priests, that is, who literally did nothing but recite the Mass because they had no training and did not know how to preach. Deprived of solid doctrine this way, the laity took on bad doctrines, often spread by teachers who were simply ignorant. Sub-Christian notions crept back in and distorted Catholic teaching.

The Church's perfectly sound traditions about the correct use of sacramentals, for instance, were allowed to mix with leftovers from Europe's recently dead pagan past. Sacred medals became charms; relics were confused with rabbit's feet. In a disaster area like this, with no time to spare for jumping through moral or theological hoops, quick cures were needed—so the Church became a source for magic pills, not spiritual salvation. Doctors and theologians kept the true teaching on the books, to be sure, but popular extravagances happened far away from the universities. "For instance," as Belloc writes,

> the doctrine of the Invocation of Saints is clear; but towards the end of the Middle Ages you get men robbing one shrine to enrich another. The doctrine of the use of Masses is clear, and especially their use for the benefit of the souls in Purgatory; but the superstition that a Mass in this place was efficacious, and in that was not—the superstition which confuses mechanical repetition with spiritual force grew as the Middle Ages declined.[23]

Somewhat akin to this are the many fantastic legends about the saints and the early Church that grew up during these years,

---

[23] Ibid., 81.

based, in many cases, on few, if any, historical facts. Most of them were perhaps harmless — saints who never existed, shrines built at the sites of miracles that never happened — harmless, that is, until they came to be confused with the actual tenets of the Faith. Laypeople lost the ability to distinguish between actual Sacred Tradition and tradition with a small *t* (i.e., just old, oft-repeated stories, many times nothing but wives' tales). Worse, both sets of ideas came to be held with the same tenacity — leaving the Resurrection of Our Blessed Lord in the same category with St. George's dragon.

And then, a few decades later, when some Lollard or Lutheran came along, bringing proofs against the "Donation of Constantine" or the "False Decretals," many a vulnerable papist joined the Protestants in their Bible-only beliefs, convinced that they had now seen the folly of "man-made" Christianity.

When the Black Death began to subside in the late 1300s, some measure of order was restored. Why, afterward, weren't efforts made to sort through these fables and false documents? There were — but only *after* the Protestant revolt. Before then, there was simply too little incentive to overcome the inertia. And here, of course, is where the bad shepherds returned big time. Too much money was being generated by this point, money the Church had come to depend on. The best example is the most famous: the sale of indulgences, against which Luther wrote his Ninety-Five Theses.

There's some legitimate question about whether the indulgence seller who prompted Luther's protest really understood the nature of indulgences as put forward in official Church doctrine; his sponsor, however, Pope Leo X, certainly must have.

The actual teaching, though it has an unaccustomed sound today, isn't terribly difficult to understand — but it does require a good deal of faith in the Church's ability to draw out correctly the implications of her own core beliefs. Spiritual goods merited by the saints are stored up with God as in a treasury. These treasures, under certain circumstances, can be applied to the needs of other Church members still on earth—and the pope, as successor of Peter, holds the keys.

What kinds of needs are we talking about? The need, for instance, to have the sufferings brought about by our own sins and follies lessened.

Here's an important point, though, and one that was often lost in the controversy: an indulgence can be granted only to *a living, baptized Christian believer*. It's of no use for keeping someone out of hell, for that issue is settled only by graces earned by Christ Himself applied directly to the believing soul in baptism. Post-baptismal sin, too, is absolved not by an indulgence but by confession.

The indulgences offered by the Church were (and still are) useful for mitigating *troubles in time*—temporal chastisement here on earth during the struggle for sanctification and, if necessary, in the purging that comes to a saved soul immediately after death.

One more thing: the idea that an indulgence obtained by a living believer might, on his own authority, be transferred to *a third party* (a deceased loved one in purgatory, for example) was a theory sometimes entertained but *never actually taught by the Church*. Pope Leo, again, certainly understood all this—but he also knew that these fine distinctions, during those troubled times, were well over the heads of the Catholic masses.

Even so, he sent out his authorized sellers. Johann Tetzel, for example, was a German Dominican friar engaged to preach the great indulgence of 1517, a campaign undertaken (ostensibly) to help finance the construction of the largest church building on earth, the new St. Peter's going up in Rome. Tetzel had been at this kind of work for some time already, having been commissioned by Pope Leo (while he was still Cardinal Giovanni de' Medici) to boost the Jubilee Indulgence more than a decade earlier. He had achieved great results. Tetzel was valued as a rousing street preacher, somebody who could "fill a hat" like practically no one else — but his technique was highly suspect. Later charges that he preached "indulgence" in our modern sense are slanderous, anachronistic nonsense. *Indulgentia* (a Latin word that may be rendered as "a kindness going forward") was not, as so many Protestants have charged, a bribe offered to God by the impenitent, so that He might "go easy" or "look the other way" during the commission of future sins. And Tetzel probably did not use the silly advertising jingle so often associated with his name: "As soon as the coin in the coffer clinks, the soul from purgatory springs!" But he definitely promoted the same idea in subtler language. "The assertion," as Catholic historian Ludwig von Pastor writes,

> that he put forward indulgences as being not only a remission of the temporal punishment of sin, but as a remission of its guilt, is as unfounded as is that other accusation against him, that he sold the forgiveness of sin for money, without even any mention of contrition and confession, or that, for payment, he absolved from sins which might be committed in the future.... About indulgences for the living, Tetzel always taught pure doctrine.... The case was very different, however, with indulgences for the dead. About these there is no doubt that Tetzel did, according to what he considered his authoritative instructions, proclaim as Christian doctrine that nothing but an offering of

money was required to gain the indulgence for the dead, without there being any question of contrition or confession. He also taught, in accordance with the opinion then held, that an indulgence could be applied to any given soul with unfailing effect. Starting from this assumption, there is no doubt that his doctrine was virtually that of the well-known drastic proverb.[24]

When Tetzel arrived at Wittenberg in Saxony, word of his message reached Martin Luther, who was an important teacher of theology at the Catholic university there. The ordinary people who attended the rallies, Luther claimed (and there's no real reason to disbelieve him), came away from Tetzel's preaching convinced that they could free their loved ones from purgatory purely for a price. Luther wrote to his bishop, Albert of Brandenburg, to protest. And here's where things got dicey. Tetzel had received his license to preach in the pope's name via this selfsame archbishop of Brandenburg, who had, as it happens, arranged with Leo in advance to send him about *half* the money raised, for the construction project in Rome—and to keep the other half himself to pay off the deep debts he incurred while obtaining his appointment to the archbishopric. This the ordinary people did not know. And Albert himself, once he received the letter, went after Luther, the whistle-blower.

Luther probably didn't know about this bad shepherd's abuse either; there's no specific mention of it, at any rate, in the Ninety-Five Theses, which focus almost entirely on theology. We know about it today, however, and it highlights like nothing else one

[24] Ludwig von Pastor, *The History of the Popes, from the Close of the Middle Ages*, ed. Ralph Francis Kerr (London: Kegan Paul, Trench, Trubner, 1908), 7.

of the major reasons the clergy were so resistant to reform during these crucial years. They were convinced that the Church needed the money to continue. The popes had, for decades, given their sanction to similar transactions quite openly, and in exchange for a fee. Even secular rulers had a hand in perpetuating the festering mess because large indulgence rallies like Tetzel's generated money for local economies like a big football championship—merchants, innkeepers, and the like, and burgomasters, city councilmen, and so forth often received a cut from "civic-minded" groups. The whole thing stank like a garbage dump.

Luther wasn't the only one who cried foul about the theology. His later opponent Cardinal Thomas Cajetan, sent to reclaim Luther for the Faith in 1518, had been protesting the same irresponsible preaching for years—and Cajetan definitely *did* know where the money went: "Preachers," he said,

> speak in the name of the Church only so long as they proclaim the doctrine of Christ and His Church; but if, *for purposes of their own*, they teach that about which they know nothing, and which is only their own imagination, they must not be accepted as mouthpieces of the Church. No one must be surprised if such as these fall into error.[25]

To put it bluntly, an indulgence preacher who kept it simple ("As soon as the coin in the coffer clinks ...") ginned up cash a lot faster than a careful theologian, and so Brother Love's Traveling Salvation Show was suffered to continue.

None of this should, of course, be taken as a defense for Martin Luther's later revolution. The apostles established a Church with "one Lord, one Faith, one baptism" (Eph. 4:5), which no

[25] Ibid., 7.

man is justified in sundering, no matter how many Judases stain her offices or how infuriating their offenses. Benedict Arnold, in other words, is no less a traitor if America really did have crimes of her own to atone for and abuses (such as slavery) as yet unreformed.

But not just any old stick is good enough to beat Martin Luther with; and the abuse he overreacted to was no less an abuse because his own later crimes were also great. It does not seem to have occurred to Pope Leo, after all, that he might easily have paid off St. Peter's to the glory of God by liquidating his own luxuries and those of his equally profligate Curia. That same Leo once said (if the legend is true), "Since God has given us the papacy, let us enjoy it."

Finally, we come to the *Hundred Years' War*—the third of our great precipitating disasters. This event (actually a series of small, closely related wars that lasted a little more than a century) overlapped both the Great Schism and the Black Death, blurring the whole miserable fourteenth century into one long nightmare. The causes of the war, to put things much too simply, arose from the Great Schism, a rift that allowed the French and the English to begin quarrelling over their mutual (and equally legitimate) claims to the throne of William the Conqueror. Several familiar names fought on one side or the other, including, most notably, St. Joan of Arc for the French and, for the English, King Henry V, made immortal by Shakespeare. As with most wars, this one spread poverty, sickness, and despair as if it were a clever engine created to produce just those results. It also emphasized *national identity* in a Europe that, up to then, had been pervaded by a common Catholic identity. Along with the nasty little "War of the Eight Saints," which helped bring the Avignon papacy to an end, the Hundred Years' War seemed to many to give the lie at last to Christianity's great pretentions as the bringer of peace on earth.

To employ a bit of a frivolous metaphor, it appears to have been to medieval Christendom just what the breakup of the Beatles was to the vaunted Age of Aquarius. "'All You Need Is Love'? Love couldn't even keep the Beatles together." Similarly, in the fourteenth century, Catholicism seemed impotent against man's worst instincts; at times, it even seemed to exacerbate them. Popes who once settled international disputes were now in the thick of the action.

Nationalism was born. As we saw at Avignon, the churches of the various nations linked their interests more and more to those of their own secular princes, less and less to the leadership in Rome. Constant war finally "militarized" the whole medieval mind-set. Rulers, both civil and religious, became *authoritarians*. Once again, Belloc explains it well:

> The use of force, punishment, threat and fear are neces-
> sary for the keeping of order and the maintenance of right
> laws in action. But in a healthy state of affairs, much the
> greater part in the strength of authority is moral. Men
> obey because they think they ought to obey; because they
> feel that the authority which governs them has a right to
> do so. As moral authority weakens, those who exercise
> authority tend to fall back upon physical restraint, punish-
> ment, and the irrational fear of consequences as a method
> of administration. That is what happened towards the end
> of the Middle Ages. Force alone was used against heresy in
> every form, and not only against heresy but even against
> grumblings at the powers of the clergy.... Everywhere
> attacked and losing [their] moral sanctions, the officers

of the Church fell back with increasing severity and frequency upon restraint by fear. This evil, the association of violence and horrible punishment with the maintenance of orthodoxy, grew rapidly throughout the end of the decline; and nothing did more to provoke the violent outburst to follow, in which the unity of Christendom was broken asunder.[26]

Here, a single illustration may stand in for the many examples that could be cited. Jan Hus was a Czech priest who served as rector of Charles University in Prague at the turn of the fifteenth century. Actual Protestantism was still more than a hundred years off, but Hus, who lived and died a Catholic, gradually became interested in the writings of John Wycliffe. Clergy mortality from the Black Death had been especially high in England, and Wycliffe, the master of Balliol College, had seen all the worst men in Oxfordshire rise to the Catholic episcopate. His simmering fury over the whole thing began expressing itself in books that eventually reached Bohemia.

Unlike his teacher, Hus did not respond to the scandals by attacking the dogma of transubstantiation (which, after all, does depend on a validly ordained priesthood). But he did begin to share Wycliffe's Donatist beliefs that the Catholic clergy had relinquished all its prerogatives through sin and simony.

Hus's remedy?

The Church ought to sell off the entirety of her property and make the whole clergy take a vow of abject poverty. Indulgences and the like must be banned, and the Bible must become Christianity's sole guidebook.

---

[26] Belloc, *The Crisis of Civilization*, 86.

In 1377, Hus published his ideas, which quickly earned the condemnation of Pope Gregory XI. A few years later, Innocent VII censured Hus and forbade any further broadsides against the clergy. By 1409, Hus's sympathetic archbishop was forced to stop protecting him. Another new pope was elected, antipope Alexander V, and Hus decided to appeal to him directly, offering to explain his teachings in person. He was rebuffed. In 1412, his followers burned the papal bulls that had been issued against Hus. Three of them were taken and beheaded. King Wenceslaus of Bohemia tried to intervene and almost got into hot water himself with Gregory XII.

Finally, Jan Hus was sent to trial. Yet another antipope, John XXIII, chose a committee of bishops to adjudicate the matter. Hus's condemnation took place on June 5, 1415. He was held for another seventy-three days and then burned alive, the same punishment Wycliffe underwent some twenty years earlier. Before being consigned to the flames, he prayed the Jesus Prayer and forgave his enemies. He was undoubtedly a heretic—as some in our times have become through shock and dismay—but when he said that indulgences had become a colossal fraud, that the monasteries were rotten with idleness and sexual sin, and that the bishops, for the most part, were in it for the money, Jan Hus told the God's honest truth.

Which bad shepherd in this very unedifying story shall we pick for our final goat? There's an embarrassment of "riches," of course, but whichever candidate we choose, the story will end up being a rerun. Gregory XI, first to tangle with Wycliffe, was the last of the Avignon popes. Innocent VII was one of the rival popes during the Great Schism; he hushed up Hus's charges of nepotism in the Church and then made his own worthless nephew captain of the papal militia not long afterward, nearly causing a war. Alexander V, in whose name the three Hussites were beheaded, wasn't even a pope at all but one of the French-sponsored antipopes. Gregory XII was soon deposed by the Council of Constance. And Hus was burned on the authority of John XXIII—who actually had no authority, since he, too, was nothing but another antipope, also deposed at Constance. The killing of Hus, in other words, resulted from a perfect storm of all three of our fourteenth-century catastrophes.

John XXIII (who is, of course, not to be confused with the real, twentieth-century pontiff who called the Second Vatican Council) refused the order to abdicate, incidentally, and fled the city disguised as a postman. When he was finally captured and tried for heresy and immorality, he was found guilty on all counts. As the historian Gibbon adds, "The more scandalous charges were suppressed; the 'vicar of Christ' was accused only of piracy, rape, sodomy, murder, and incest."[27] John was also convicted of simony and schism; but, if you don't mind another pop-culture reference, we might paraphrase Martin Sheen's Captain Willard in *Apocalypse Now*: "Charging a man with simony and schism in this place was like handing out speeding tickets at the Indy 500."

[27] Edward Gibbon, *The Decline and Fall of the Roman Empire*, vol. 6 (London: A. Strahan, 1802), 243.

Chapter 4

The Catholic Protestants:
The Great Sixteenth-Century Rebels—
and Those Who Drove Them to Revolt

It ought to go without saying, but all the men who created Protestantism were Catholics.

Wycliffe and Hus, as we've seen, were both Catholic university professors (and ordained priests, to boot). Luther was a doctor of theology at the Catholic University in Wittenberg and was eventually made vicar of Saxony and Thuringia, overseer of eleven monasteries. Theodore Beza, his successor as the head of Lutheranism, was a canon lawyer from Paris. Ulrich Zwingli was a Swiss priest who was awarded a pension by Pope Julius II (patron of Michelangelo) for taking the papal side in the politics of the day. John Calvin was a French seminarian who quit school and turned to law when his father, a cathedral notary, was fired on suspicions of embezzlement. William Farel, who persuaded Calvin to return to Geneva, had worked with pro-reform priests at the University of Paris before throwing up his hands in the end and joining the Protestants. King Henry VIII of England topped them all, having composed early in his reign an anti-Protestant apologetic called *Defense of the Seven Sacraments*—which also includes a spirited defense of papal supremacy! In fact, Henry was, in consequence, awarded the title of *Fidei Defensor* (Defender of the Faith) by Pope Leo X, an honorific that has not been surrendered by his Protestant successors, not even to this day. And Henry, before his own defection, hated Lutherans with a passion and ordered them hanged, burned, and whipped out of his realm.

The other Catholics — the ones, that is, who worked to suppress their new movement — were, of course, on the correct side. Heresy — "the obstinate post-baptismal denial of some truth which must be believed with divine and catholic faith"[28] — is a sin. Leading others into heresy is a very grievous sin. "A man that is a heretic," as the old Douay Bible puts it, "after the first and second admonition, avoid: knowing that ... such an one is subverted, and sinneth, being condemned by his own judgment" (Titus 3:10–11). St. Paul had other things to say on this topic as well, as, for instance, when he insisted that

> the Lord's servant must not be quarrelsome but kindly to everyone, an apt teacher, forbearing, correcting his opponents with gentleness. God may perhaps grant that they will repent and come to know the truth, and they may escape from the snare of the devil, after being captured by him to do his will. (2 Tim. 2:24–26)

Note the apostolic command: the Lord's servant *must* be kindly, forbearing, gentle. St. James adds an important thought, too: "God opposes the proud but gives grace to the humble" (4:6) — and, as several wise persons have added since, He opposes the proud even when they happen to be right.

Our next set of bad shepherds then, comes in *two classes*: men who turned on the Church for not reforming herself fast enough

---

[28] *Catechism of the Catholic Church*, no. 2089.

and then tried to cope with their resulting excommunication by explaining it away via new theology; and unreformed Church leaders who, by their high-handed arrogance, pitiless cruelty, and insufferable hypocrisy, goaded the protesters deeper and deeper into their follies.

It's anachronistic and unhistorical to speak of "the Catholics and the Protestants" in these early stages. They're all Catholics: some fully in revolt; others in the right theologically but really defending the abuses in which they were vested. And there were also a few honest, bewildered Catholic souls in the middle, trying not to get swept away by it all—men, as we shall see, like Cajetan, Staupitz, Melanchthon, and More. The Reformation, in other words, was a perfectly preventable civil war in the Household of God that ended—as our own War between the States did not—in the recognition of two seemingly permanent, independent, and antagonistic domains.

Martin Luther, God help him, probably suffered from mental health problems; many experts who have studied his early writings feel that he displays there all the classic signs of obsessive-compulsive disorder (OCD). He was, at the very least, a morbidly introspective, deeply melancholy young man.

"Like many a hundred others of his time, Luther was a friar who should never have been a friar," writes historian Philip Hughes; his original decision, in fact, to join the Augustinians was made in haste, after Luther was struck (or nearly so) by lightning during a terrible thunderstorm. Once committed to the order, he chose the strictest monastery available and plunged himself into a severe regimen of silence and almost constant fasting. The theology he learned there, as Hughes continues, "was superficial in the extreme. His only guides were the scholastics of the decay, Nominalist in tendency, and, in fact, convinced of the impossibility of any synthesis of reason and faith."[29] Luther found a brief respite once he was ordained as a priest, a real season of grace in which he experienced considerable comfort and peace with God. Alas, it passed, and his scrupulosity resurfaced stronger than ever. "He suffered terrible trials and anguish of spirit," writes Thomas Bokenkotter, "with sudden spasms of terror and despair gripping his heart, a torment so shattering, he said, that had it lasted the tenth part of an hour his bones would have crumbled into ashes.... Craving certainty, he confessed frequently, even daily, fasted and prayed; but he found little relief."[30] His confessor Johann von Staupitz, vicar-general of his order, tried to help; and Luther himself admits, "If it had not been for Dr. Staupitz, I should have sunk in hell."[31]

Even so, Luther was not really released. One of the most distinctive traits of OCD is the intrusive thoughts to which sufferers feel compelled to give vent and which afterward produce self-loathing. Once, when Dr. Staupitz tried to cut through his terrors by insisting that the baptized believer need only pray the Our Father and love God, Luther cried out, "But I don't love God. I hate him!"[32]

Not surprisingly, the young Augustinian delved deeply into the writings of Augustine during this period—especially that great Father's controversies with the Pelagians. If Luther really

---

[29] Philip Hughes, *A Popular History of the Catholic Church* (Garden City, NY: Image Books, 1954), 163.

[30] Bokenkotter, *A Concise History*, 187.

[31] See Dan Graves, MSL, "Johann von Staupitz, Luther's Confessor," Christianity.com, June 2007, https://www.christianity.com/church/church-history/timeline/1501-1600/johann-von-staupitz-luthers-confessor-11629932.html.

[32] See ibid.

was suffering from OCD, as suspected, this probably wasn't a good idea. In countering Pelagian insistence that man's return to God is initiated by man himself and undertaken on his own strength, Augustine reemphasized the words of Christ Himself: "You did not choose me, but I chose you and appointed you that you should go and bear fruit and that your fruit should abide" (John 15:16). From here, Augustine worked out an entire theology of prevenient grace that seems, at times, to venture perilously close to a full denial of free will, rendering mankind completely inert, never acting but only being acted upon. And here the tormented Luther at last pricked up his ears.

Augustine himself, who seems at times to have been a little appalled at the implications of his own thought, had always been careful to avow his willingness to leave the final judgment of his works to the Church in union with the pope. Luther, living twelve hundred years downstream from his tutor and in a very polluted part of the river, felt significantly less inclined to trust the Church's judgment—especially now that the idea of inert helplessness began to sound like such a blessed relief!

At the time, Luther expressed it (in a passage beloved by Protestants) as simply coming to understand the true gospel: "At last, by the mercy of God, by meditating day and night, I gave heed to those words [of St. Paul], namely, 'He who through faith is righteous shall live' [Gal. 3:11]. Here I felt that I was altogether born again and had entered paradise itself through open gates. Here a totally other face of the entire Scripture showed itself to me."

Later, however, in a book called *The Bondage of the Will*, Luther spelled out exactly which aspect of this idea had comforted him so much:

> I say that man, before he is renewed into the new creation
> of the Spirit's kingdom, does and endeavors nothing to

prepare himself for that new creation and kingdom, and even after he is re-created does and endeavors nothing towards his perseverance in that kingdom; the Spirit alone works both blessings in us, regenerating us, and preserving us when regenerate, without ourselves.

The mere experiencing of "faith," in other words, accomplishes everything and thus brings life; and not just for those receiving their initial re-creation at baptism (at which point the statement is true as it stands) but also for the Christian believer going forward.

Omnipotence and the foreknowledge of God utterly destroy the doctrine of "free-will" … and I frankly confess that, for myself, even if it could be, I should not want "free-will" to be given me, nor anything to be left in my own hands. … In that case, I should still be forced to labor with no guarantee of success. But now God has taken my salvation out of the control of my own will and put it under the control of His.[33]

Resting now in the peace of his own passivity — in his new-found realization that no one can either please or displease God in any way unless God Himself has willed it so — Luther became a new man. He began to teach his liberating ideas to his students at the university. Many people don't quite realize how long Luther preached his distinctive message *inside the Catholic Church* — and with hardly any trouble from the authorities. His "revolutionary" ideas, as we've seen, diverged little, if at all, from

---

[33] Martin Luther, *The Bondage of the Will* (Grand Rapids, MI: Revell, 1957), 313–314.

certain familiar aspects of Augustinian theology commonplace since the fourth century.

Documents discovered only in the twentieth century, in fact, show that Luther was developing his "conversion" insight *at least four years before* the famous crisis moment of 1517, in lectures on the Psalms he delivered to his students in Wittenberg. "How compatible Luther's theology actually was with Catholic tradition," continues Bokenkotter,

> is a question that has been debated ever since. There is no doubt that there was something new and original in Luther's theology; it was highly personal and charged with emotion — in sharp contrast with the cold, dry, Scholastic treatises of the day. Unlike too many presentations at that time, it was also profoundly biblical. It was also a practical and relevant theology, which focused on the actual issues of the day, and this contributed to its cachet of novelty. But none of these characteristics tell against it being accepted as basically Catholic.[34]

There's just no telling, in fact, how long Martin Luther might have continued to emphasize his emphasis in peace, had not Johann Tetzel appeared, paying off Archbishop Albert's debts.

As Chesterton once put it so memorably, "The reformer is always right about what is wrong. He is generally wrong about what is right." This expresses, really, the whole tragedy of the Reformation.

> Like all enlightened men of the age, Luther was fully aware of the terrible state of the Church; his sermons before 1517

---

[34] Bokenkotter, *A Concise History*, 197.

are sufficient indication of this. Like others he complained of the avarice, simony and ecclesiastical jobbery connected with appointment to high and low office in the Church. But there is no indication that he felt these abuses warranted revolutionary action—until he became convinced that the Gospel itself was at stake, that the Church was betraying the Gospel of Jesus Christ by teaching people that heaven could be purchased by good works.[35]

When Luther's students came to him, believing that Tetzel was teaching the Church's own doctrine at his outlandish rallies, he was right in perceiving the need for action; he was certainly wrong, however, in believing that his own new patent medicine ("the bondage of the will") was just what the doctor ordered.

The iconic image of Luther nailing his anti-Tetzel theses to the Wittenberg castle door may or may not represent a real event; most historians think he simply delivered them to the archbishop who had licensed the indulgence seller. And it was only when Albert—yes, that same bad shepherd, the archbishop of Brandenburg, who needed to repay the three hundred thousand ducats he had borrowed to get a waiver for holding three bishoprics at once!—disdained to return his call, so to speak, that Luther got riled. He distributed the Ninety-Five Theses publicly (using the recently invented Gutenberg printing press, by the way) and challenged all comers to debate.

Even then, however, his purpose was *not* to break with the Church, much less to start a new religion.

Another common misconception is the notion that the Theses spelled out Luther's whole well-known later program:

---

[35] Ibid., 191.

faith alone, Scripture alone, "The pope is the Antichrist," and so forth. No, the original document, once again, dealt solely with the issues surrounding indulgences (though some of them do tangentially call one or two aspects of papal authority into question).

The other ideas were simmering in his mind, to be sure, and perhaps in the minds of his students; but not even now, here on the very first Reformation Day (October 31, 1517), had Luther become the imperious Promethean of later years: he's still just a Catholic professor who wants to talk.

His theology had started a stir with his colleagues, sure enough, "but such academic skirmishes had little interest for the public at large. It was only when he attacked the Church's system of indulgences—which touched the life of almost everyone—that the whole world began to listen in."[36]

It blew up overnight.

Suddenly, Luther's name was on everyone's lips, clerical or lay, poor or rich. Here, at last, was a man not afraid to speak truth to power, as the modern phrase would have it. Metaphorically, the whole German Volk took Luther onto their shoulders like the quarterback who just tossed the game-winning pass. For a bookish fellow who had until recently been just another guilt-ridden nobody closeted away with monks, it was heady stuff indeed.

It must have been a nasty shock, however, when Luther learned that his fame (or infamy, depending on whom you asked) reached Pope Leo X in Rome as well. His status as one of the Catholic Protestants is fully on display in the letter Luther addressed to the pope on May 30, 1518:

[36] Ibid.

I know, most holy father, that evil reports are being spread about me, some friends having vilified me to your Holiness, as if I were trying to belittle the power of the Keys and of the Supreme Pontiff.... I am being accused of being a heretic, a renegade; and a thousand other ill names are being hurled at me, enough to make my ears tingle and my eyes start in my head, but my one source of confidence is an innocent conscience.... Some time ago the preaching of the apostolic jubilee of the Indulgences was begun, and soon made such headway that these preachers thought they could say what they wished, under the shelter of your Holiness's name, alarming the people with malicious, heretical lies ... [causing] the power of the Keys and the Pope being spoken evil of in Germany. And when I heard of such things, I burned with zeal for the honor of Christ, or, if some will have it so, the young blood within me boiled and yet I felt it did not behoove me to do anything in the matter except to draw the attention of some prelates to the abuses. Some acted upon the hint, but others derided it, and interpreted it in various ways.[37]

This, by the way, was all perfectly true. The archbishop still showed no interest in Luther's red flag beyond the hint that his tax repayments might be hindered by it. Tetzel himself was still ignoring Luther's call to debate and still stumping for shekels. "Tetzel's brother Dominicans," adds Bokenkotter,

> narrowed down the whole issue immediately to one of authority and in effect told Luther to accept the whole

---

[37] *The Letters of Martin Luther*, ed. Margaret A. Currie (London: Macmillan, 1908), 28–29.

system of indulgences without cavil or be burned as a heretic. The only occasion for calm debate was furnished by Luther's fellow Augustinians at their chapter in Heidelberg, on April 26, 1518, where Luther won over the majority to his views."[38]

"From this, most holy father," as Luther concludes his letter,

has such a fire been kindled, that, to judge from the hue and cry, one would think the whole world had been set ablaze.... So, to reconcile my opponents if possible, and satisfy the expectations of many ... I made [my theses] public that I might have the protection of your Holiness's name, and find refuge beneath the shadow of your wings. Therefore, most holy father, I prostrate myself at your feet, placing myself and all I am and have at your disposal, to be dealt with as you see fit.... Come what may, I shall recognize the voice of your Holiness to be that of Christ, speaking through you."[39]

Not long after receiving this, Pope Leo famously told his advisers that the whole thing was obviously nothing but a tiff between idle monks and went back to "more important" matters. Luther's appeals for papal adjudication went unanswered.

When, a year or so later, the kerfuffle finally got too loud to tune out anymore, the pope, forced to interrupt his pressing affairs, simply threw a fit—there's nothing else to call it. Having heard rumors that the man occasionally got carried away and spoke of "an evil spirit hovering over Rome," Leo ordered the

---

[38] Bokenkotter, *A Concise History*, 193.
[39] *The Letters of Martin Luther*, 31.

troublesome German to appear there in person within sixty days to face a charge of heresy.

The document, drawn up by the papal theologian Sylvester Prierias, includes not a single word of recognition that Luther's concerns about abuse had a scrap of validity. It does include a long string of personal insults, added at the end of the summons in the pontiff's own hand: Luther is "a loathsome fellow ... the son of a bitch, born to bite and snap at the sky ... with a brain of brass and a nose of iron," no more welcome in the papal palace than a leper.[40] St. Peter, of course, had welcomed lepers and healed them during his term as Vicar of Christ; but that recollection appears to have slipped Leo's mind for the moment.

And just like that, Dr. Martin Luther's career as a Catholic university professor was over. The pope had called him a fool, and there's just no recovering from that in Luther's line of work. For Luther now, it was either beg in the streets or double down and take the whole thing to another level. His many fans practically made the decision for him.

What saved Luther's life at this point is simple to explain. The pope was undergoing yet another of those uncomfortable periods during which he had to fear the power of the Holy Roman emperor. The Curia needed the help of Frederick, elector of Saxony, to keep him on their side — and Frederick had already become interested in Martin Luther's message; yes, he was another Catholic Protestant.

So Luther stayed in Germany, and the pope sent a man to Augsburg to meet "the dog with the brain of brass." A couple of centuries earlier, the pope would have called a crusade against

---

[40] Quoted in J. Todd, *Martin Luther* (Glen Rock, NJ: Paulist Press, 1964), 147.

any Christian prince who dared to come between a heretic and the Holy See. But now, as Belloc writes:

> The day for crusades was ended. Expediency and politics, not principle, governed the movement of Catholic armies. Even the pope did not wish to offend Luther's sovereign. And to the very end the Catholic princes would not support the emperor in a war against the Lutheran princes, lest a Catholic victory might help towards that restoration of the imperial power in the empire which they dreaded more than anything else.[41]

Cardinal Thomas Cajetan was the man sent to obtain Luther's recantation, but their debate was, even in the eyes of very orthodox observers, something of a draw — more testimony, surely, to the fact that, when calmly expressed, most of Luther's ideas were still within the pale at this point.

Luther did, however, when very tired near the end, let slip a remark questioning the limits of papal jurisdiction. It was enough to condemn him had Cajetan's sponsors been so inclined, but, at the moment, carrying him out of Germany would have been politically difficult. Luther slipped away instead, and the process petered out for the time being.

A later debate, at Leipzig in July 1519, showed Luther's amazing popularity beginning to go to his head. There, he allowed a more antagonistic theologian, Johann Eck, to corner him into what seemed an outright denial of what he had affirmed in his letter to Leo a year before: that the power of the keys belongs to the supreme pontiff.

---

[41] Belloc, *The Crisis of Civilization*, 98.

The rest can, and perhaps should, be told quickly. Luther wrote books while the pope and the Curia wrung their hands. The first book was borderline defensible, consisting of the usual call to reform the usual abuses, but also going beyond that to take definite stands on widely debated, not quite heretical matters, such as the celibacy of the clergy and limits to the pope's temporal jurisdiction.

A second book went further, crossing over into genuine Donatist errors inherited from Wycliffe and a denial of apostolic succession. And all during this deadly interregnum, when political Rome was too timid to act, Luther's supporters egged him on —drove him, like a stunt performer, to add ever more dangerous feats to his act.

A little kindness at any time, a little more sympathy for the genuine and urgent concerns that started him out, from a man supposed to be his Holy Father in Christ Jesus might have prevented one of the great world tragedies. Instead, Pope Leo came down harshly on a fragile man clearly in over his head, calling him a son of a bitch for no reason other than irritation at being called out, with no middle ground in between, even though there was middle ground aplenty to be explored, as Cajetan and Staupitz seem willing to grant. "The growing rebellion," according to Belloc, "was met by lawyers' tricks, by the use of force, by continued and often fearful punishments, but not by that spiritual change, that repentance which the times demanded."[42] One bad shepherd fueled a conflagration that should have been avoided.

On June 15, 1520, Pope Leo issued the bull *Exsurge Domine*, which condemned forty-one of Luther's propositions. Eck took

[42] Belloc, *The Crisis of Civilization*, 98.

it to Germany and was almost lynched. The people wouldn't have any of his bull—they took it away from him and burned it. Luther, of course, responded to their new incitements with increased fanaticism: he designated the pope, for the first time publicly, as the Antichrist.

Incredibly, many historians feel that, even then, the Rubicon had not yet been crossed.

There was much confusion over the exact issues, and the multitude of alternatives was bewildering. Some felt that all could be settled if only certain ecclesiastical abuses were straightened out. Others pointed to the theological disagreements as crucial but could not agree on their relative importance. The papal bull *Exsurge* seemed to assert that Luther's main errors concerned penance and indulgences, but [the sixteenth-century scholar] Erasmus considered free will the main issue. The humanist scholar Melanchthon was persuaded at Augsburg in 1520 that unity could be restored if only priests were allowed to marry and the chalice given back to the laity. Luther himself maintained that it was all about the proper understanding of Christ. And where did justification by faith alone fit in? Many who accepted Luther's understanding of the Gospel didn't feel it necessary to reject the old Church. Papal primacy, for instance, was still highly controversial within the Roman Church itself.... As late as 1530 there was still general optimism about the possibility of reconciliation. [The emperor] Charles scheduled a diet for Augsburg for that year, and Melanchthon, [now] Luther's closest associate, who still considered himself a Catholic, drew up a confession, still the official basis of

Lutheranism, which indicated only accidental differences with traditional Catholicism.[43]

Bad shepherds—and in this category we must now include, without qualification, Luther himself—spoiled everything, however. Five years and one *Deutscher Bauernkrieg* (Great Peasants' Revolt—a war in which roughly two hundred thousand Germans perished miserably) later, the cycle of folly had done its dirty deed. Two centuries of unheeded pleas, of contempt for "lay interference" in ecclesiastical matters, had filled a gigantic Pandora's box with violence and insanity, and Luther, in the arrogance of his newfound celebrity, flung the box open with reckless abandon.

If he had been a sympathetic character once, Luther by now had transformed himself completely into the very thing he hated. "Let everyone who can, smite, slay, and stab them, secretly and openly," he raved, when the peasants of Thuringia took his own attitude toward authority too far:

> They have sworn to be true and faithful, submissive and obedient, to their rulers [the new Lutheran princes of Germany] ... but now they are deliberately and violently breaking this oath.... They are starting a rebellion and are violently robbing and plundering monasteries and castles which are not theirs.... They cloak this terrible and horrible sin with the gospel.... Fine Christians they are! I think there is not a devil left in hell; they have all gone into the peasants.[44]

---

[43] Bokenkotter, *A Concise History*, 193.

[44] *Against the Murderous, Thieving Hordes of Peasants*, in Martin Luther, *Documents of Modern History*, trans. E. G. Rupp and Benjamin Drewery (London: Edward Arnold, 1970), 121–126.

Later, he took full credit once the nobles had followed his advice: "I, Martin Luther, have during the rebellion slain all the peasants, for it was I who ordered them to be struck dead." And once excommunicated, the insults Luther directed against the pope made Leo's own of 1519 seem like the work of an amateur:

> You vulgar boor, blockhead, and lout, you ass to cap all asses, screaming your heehaws.... You are the scum of all the scoundrels.... I would not dream of judging or punishing you, except to say that you were born from the backside of the devil, are full of devils, lies, blasphemy, and idolatry.... If this makes you furious, you can do something in your pants and hang it around your neck.

Payback was hell—for all of us, in a world wracked by religious chaos ever since.

That chaos reached the Reformers themselves in a remarkably short time. All had been united for a season by their common fury against papal hypocrisy, the long resistance to reform. Soon it became clear that each of them would now insist on bringing his own brand of reform—and let the other guys get with *his* program. The Protestants are quite right to say that Luther hadn't really wanted a new church, though he certainly did found one in the end. He just felt that he'd make a better pope than the pope, which, to be honest, wasn't such an unreasonable belief, given the rogues' gallery of pontifical malefactors reviewed so far in these pages. Luther had never wanted *no authority* in matters of religion (as the war on the anarchic peasants so vividly demonstrates); he just wanted better authority, biblical authority, which, for him and in practice, meant Luther's authority. And the same was true of most of the rest also.

John Calvin, still salty because of his early departure from the seminary, also needed someplace to land after burning his Catholic bridges. He wandered a couple of years, picked up Luther's writings, and learned about that glorious freedom that comes through bondage of the will. Calvin, however, with his lawyerly intellect, wasn't content to write a few incidental papers on the subject. Instead of nailing theses or protesting to bishops, Calvin sat down to write. And what he wrote probably saved Protestantism.

Luther had been a *feeling*, not a thought. When he ranted, he ranted volcanically; but at times, he also expressed, we must admit, a great deal of genuinely stirring Christian piety. The German people did not love him for nothing. He wrote hymns as well as tracts, something no one could ever imagine Calvin doing.

Instead, Calvin wrote a brilliantly reasoned exposition of Luther's original feeling—full surrender, that is, to a Christian-flavored fatalism little different from Islam—upon which a true counterchurch could be built. Known in English as *The Institutes of the Christian Religion*, "it is a book that has few rivals in the enormity of its impact on Western history and ecclesiastical and political theory."[45]

What Luther had felt, Calvin explained. Calvin was Mr. Spock to Luther's Dr. McCoy; and, as Mr. Spock did so often, Calvin probably saved the day at the last possible moment. His book was such an earthquake that he became, within just a few years, the virtual dictator of Geneva in Switzerland, recognized by Protestants and Catholics alike as "the pope of Protestantism" (unofficially, of course).

[45] Hughes, *A Popular History*, 169.

Other, "better" popes set up shop in their own respective corners of Europe and were, as we said, quite amicably pleasant with one another—at first: Zwingli in Zurich, Martin Bucer in Strasbourg, John Knox in Scotland, along with Luther in Saxony—all in a kind of loose federation together, rather like the fourteen or so autocephalous patriarchs of the Eastern Orthodox church.

Inevitably, when their talk was translated into actual governance, they all began acting, as Luther had, just like the men who had tyrannized them. Knox ruled Scotland from Edinburgh with an iron hand; and his master, Calvin, tried the eccentric freethinker Michael Servetus for heresy and convicted and murdered him—in just the same way the antipope John XXIII destroyed Hus.

How had these men come to power in these once thoroughly Catholic lands? Not discounting the unheeded cries for reform that animated vigorous minorities everywhere, the real driving force behind the changes had been that rising *nationalism* we witnessed aborning back in the fourteenth century. Where once Christian men had seen only *Christendom*, people now perceived a patchwork quilt of competing European nationalities making and breaking alliances with each other as we saw them starting to do during the Great Schism.

Former brothers and sisters in Christ living in neighboring lands were now becoming *foreigners* to each other, and no people anywhere likes to be ruled by foreigners. The princes of each nation felt this emotion as strongly as their subjects—but they felt something else, too. "As a mere negative heretical movement," reminds Belloc, "wherein a mass of divergent and even contradictory opinions had free play, the movement might have been less destructive. But there was a driving power behind it which was of very great effect: the opportunity for loot."[46] Each nation in Christendom had "great monastic establishments, the numbers enjoying which had dwindled, while their revenues had been maintained.... The Papacy was the central authority. Deny the authority of the Papacy and the vast wealth of the Church lay defenseless before attack and spoliation." Those "United Nations of Europe," which once settled their differences through the power of the papacy, now chafed under that union. Their rulers especially began to find the bridle too binding, and Protestantism became the excuse for their Declaration of Independence.

In 1529, however, the Protestant popes themselves stopped enjoying each other's company. The trigger, ironically, was the Sacrament of the Lord's Table, the very source of Christian unity in St. Paul's teaching: "Because there is one bread, we who are many are one body, for we all partake of the one bread" (1 Cor. 10:17).

Zwingli, for reasons of his own, chose to confront his role model Luther over his doctrine of the Eucharist. Though Luther had chosen to pick a fight with Rome over the word *transubstantiation*, he still held something very close to the traditional doctrine, whereas Zwingli denied the Real Presence of Christ in the Eucharist altogether, as do today's Evangelicals. Bucer and Calvin tried to mediate between the two and only made things worse. Before long, anathemas flew as they hadn't since Clement excommunicated Urban. Luther called Zwingli "a full-blown heathen." Those who agreed with him became "loathsome fanatics ... murderers of souls ... committing mortal sin ... blasphemers and enemies of Christ."[47]

---

[46] Belloc, *The Crisis of Civilization*, 100.
[47] Quoted in Dave Armstrong, *Biblical Catholic Eucharistic Theology* (n.p.: Lulu.com, 2014), 97.

According to Calvin, however, it was Luther's followers who were mad, "and in their madness, carried even [Catholic] idolatry out with them. For what else is the adorable sacrament of Luther but an idol set up in the temple of God?"[48]

A very uncomfortable conference was held at Marburg to settle the matter for all Protestants—which, of course, came to nothing. As historian Bokenkotter mildly understates it, "[Marburg] failed to bring agreement and confirmed the disquieting fact that the principle—Scripture alone—might not be sufficient to maintain a consensus." The watching world, at any rate, got the message loud and clear: this new Protestant sort of papacy came *without* the gift of infallibility.

The most naked example of this grotesque phenomenon—the strange combination of persecuting religious absolutism with confessed, indeed, self-evident fallibility—came in England in the person of the sixteenth-century archbishop of Canterbury Thomas Cranmer. It's an ugly story that deserves to be told only because it so beautifully illustrates the continuing presence of the Holy Spirit in the Church, especially in her patient, long-suffering laity.

Henry VIII was most definitely one of those princes who chafed against Europe's central authority. He also inherited an English crown that was mortgaged to the gills, a national government drowning in debt to its own richest men, the English nobility. When Pope Clement VII (not a bad shepherd himself, but weak and indecisive) finally cowboyed up and refused to

---

[48] Letter 244, to Bucer, in *Letters of John Calvin: Compiled from the Original Manuscripts and Edited with Historical Notes*, comp. Dr. Jules Bonnet, vol. 2 (Philadelphia: Presbyterian Board of Publication, 1858), 234.

grant the English king the annulment he demanded, Henry used the row as an excuse to gin up yet another schism. The schism this time, however, must not be thought of as the founding of a new Protestant nation—not to begin with, at any rate.

Henry, as we noted at the start of this chapter, disliked Protestantism intensely; he had a deep personal attachment to the Mass and allowed no theological or even liturgical changes at all during his lifetime. But he was willing to take advantage of existing ambiguities about the nature and extent of the pope's juridical rights as a way to cut Clement out of the loop *within England*. He pushed his Act of Supremacy through Parliament in 1534, declaring the English monarch, not the pope of Rome, to be supreme head of the Church in England. This left Cranmer, his still thoroughly Catholic archbishop of Canterbury, free to grant Henry the annulment that Clement had refused him. His original purpose now fulfilled, the king settled back to marry his new flame, Anne Boleyn, to raise up a fine healthy heir with her assistance, and to prove true his contention that the nation he ruled was perfectly capable of remaining *Catholic without the pope*.

Alas, the change left Henry in charge of Church finances within the English nation as well; and his own extreme straits in that area soon led him into temptation—specifically, into a temptation to break the seventh commandment. Several of the king's advisers had watched with envy while continental princes reaped a huge bounty of loot by liquidating Catholic schools and monasteries. To justify such a gigantic act of piracy, the continental Reformers produced a large mass of propaganda (some of it false, far too much of it true) about sin and scandal within these institutions.

When they showed this material to Henry, he took the bait. English convents and abbeys were despoiled; monks and nuns were turned out, the good along with the bad. In this way, the king, without really intending to do so, ensured that his schism would become permanent, since neither he nor his nobles intended ever to pay back what they had stolen or to be held accountable for the theft.

Cranmer, who, as chief cleric in the land, should have protested the loudest, was instead easily persuaded to sign off on the deal—for, as time was beginning to reveal, those who opposed Henry's schemes usually wound up in the Tower.

The most famous of Henry's advisers to take the opposite tack was noted jurist and author Sir Thomas More. Though he once briefly considered becoming a monk and eventually became a Catholic saint, More remained a layman to the end of his days, a married man and the father of four children. He was elected lord chancellor of England in 1529, the highest purely political post in the land. The trajectory which eventually brought him to the block as perhaps the king's most famous victim is very interesting indeed and hugely instructive to those of us who might need to confront clerical abuse.

More was not a naturally pugnacious man; he didn't make his famous stand because "the young blood within him had boiled." He had a warm sympathy for human frailty. He could see both sides of a story. He had, in fact, earlier been one of those very English scholars willing to question the limits of papal authority, working out a position not dissimilar to that held, once again, by the Eastern churches ("primacy of honor, not of jurisdiction") and by Luther himself at the beginning. And he was as awake to the abuses within the Church as any of the Protestants.

Thomas More, in other words, had not been spoiling for a fight. When they put him on trial for treason—for his simple unwillingness, that is, to sign the oath of royal supremacy over the Church—he stood silent for as long as possible, like His Lord before Caiaphas. He made every legitimate concession he could make. He put on no big public show. But he did stand fast on the one nonnegotiable point; and when they beheaded him for it, he became a quiet example for his fellow laypeople in times of great disorder—people like us.

Archbishop Cranmer was Thomas More's precise mirror image. The man managed flabbergasting feats of hypocrisy and dissimulation never before attempted on any stage. Though it was Henry VIII who had effectively declared himself pope in England, it was Cranmer, the Catholic archbishop, the bad shepherd, who was called upon to look the part. Over the next twenty years, it was his task to enforce, with all the brutality of the worst late-medieval pontiffs, a religious policy so ever changing and transparently political that, in the minds of English speakers and for centuries to come, it did permanent damage to the whole idea of revealed truth. Whatever might be said against capital punishment inflicted by Catholics to stop the spread of heresy, however worthy of punishment the bad Catholic shepherds themselves may have been, all of the papal violence had at least been directed against men who rebelled against the Church of their fathers, against a religion whose doctrines everyone knew and whose creeds had remained the same for more than a millennium. But inflicting hideous torments on otherwise innocent Englishmen simply because they could not, in good conscience, successfully keep up with the *orthodoxy du jour* is how Thomas Cranmer spent the remainder of his miserable existence on earth.

Henry had always persecuted Lutherans and other continental heretics; now he felt compelled to punish all English Catholics who, like More, would not sign on to his patented pope-free "catholicism."

"Amongst his tenets there were such as neither Catholics nor Protestants could, consistently with their creeds, adopt."[49] Cranmer, therefore, was called upon during the same reign to send both types of "heretic" to the stake. Henry, in fact, often made his point plain by ordering adherents of both systems carried to the place of execution *on the same wagon*, tied together in pairs back to back, "each pair containing a Catholic and a Protestant."

After Henry died, his crown was transferred to the head of his sickly son Edward. Lacking Henry's sentimental streak, the men who ruled in Edward's name knew very well that Catholicism could never be allowed to return if they were to keep either their ill-gotten loot—and their heads.

As a result, actual continental Protestantism was allowed to take root for the first time, with Calvinist, Zwinglian, and other types of preachers invited in precisely to soften the people up for further changes. "Religion, conscience, was always the pretext," writes nineteenth-century Protestant author William Cobbett,

> but in one way or another, robbery, plunder was always the end. The people, once so united and so happy, became divided into innumerable sects, no man knowing what to believe; and, indeed, no one knowing what it was lawful for him to say; for it soon became impossible for the common people to know what was heresy and what was not.

"By the end of 1549," Cobbett continues,

---

[49] This and all the remaining quotes in this chapter are from William Cobbett's *History of the Protestant Reformation in England and Ireland* (Charlotte, NC: TAN Books, 1992), 118–131.

Cranmer, who had tied so many Protestants to the stake for not being Catholics, had pretty nearly completed a system of Protestant worship. He first prepared a book of homilies and a catechism, to pave the way. Next came a law to allow the clergy to have wives ... a policy the advocating of which had merited death during the previous reign.

When questioned about this, Cranmer mildly admitted that he had privately favored the idea even while Henry was king, which must certainly have been the case, since the archbishop, as it turns out, was secretly married himself the whole time! "The infamy of Cranmer in assisting in sending people to the flames for entertaining opinions which he afterwards confessed that he himself entertained at the time that he was so sending them, can be surpassed by nothing of which human depravity is capable."

Even Cranmer, however, had trouble keeping up with the demands of the new and much more Protestant regime. "Now that prince of hypocrites, Cranmer, who, during the reign of Henry, had condemned people to the flames for not believing in transubstantiation, was ready to condemn them for believing in it." Brought in at the behest of men who had no religious opinions other than a desire to see Catholicism kept permanently out of England, the new German, Swiss, and Bohemian preachers now imported the quarrels of Luther, Calvin, and the rest to English shores. First one set rose to the top, then another — all of them empowered to make the archbishop of Canterbury do their will. "Having become openly a Protestant ... Cranmer was soon called upon to burn his fellow-Protestants, because their grounds for protesting were different from his."

To make a long, dreadful story short, Cranmer finally outsmarted himself and arranged to put his own neck into the halter. He backed the wrong horse when young Edward died, assisting in a plot to put Lady Jane Grey on the throne in usurpation of the rightful (and much more Catholic) heir, Mary Tudor.

Once again, ordinary laypeople made their opinions known. Protestantism, despite two decades of official support, had been embraced so far by only a small minority. In July 1553, large vocal protests against Lady Jane, and in favor of the rightful queen, broke out all over the country. The guinea pigs had been experimented upon long enough. Once Mary was safely crowned, most of the ringleaders were rounded up and jailed.

Mary pardoned many of them. She was convinced that the nation had come permanently to its senses once more, and she knew that any bloody retribution at this point would only make the process of healing more difficult. She may have gone too far, for she also allowed the nobles who had been enriched by the dissolution of the monasteries to go unpunished—and to keep their loot. It was, once again, intended to put the whole ugly era to bed as quickly as possible.

In exchange, the plunderers, along with the two Houses of Parliament, which had acquiesced so easily to all these crimes, made a public act of confession and recantation:

> They who, only about three or four years before, declared Cranmer's church to be 'the work of the Holy Ghost'; now these pious 'Reformation' men, having first made a firm bargain to keep the plunder, confessed that they had been guilty of a most horrible defection from the true Church; professed their sincere repentance for their past transgressions; and declared their resolution to repeal all laws enacted in prejudice of the Pope's authority!

At last, Cranmer himself was brought to trial on charges of heresy and treason in the matter of Lady Jane Grey. And now, to the surprise of no one who had been paying attention, he followed the same policy he always followed, acting on his one and only conviction: that Thomas Cranmer must save his own skin. He would sign anything, confess to anything, abjure any formerly professed belief, whatever it might take to stay out of the fires he had himself kindled so often. "He was respited for six weeks," as Cobbett tells it,

> during which time he signed six different forms of re-
> cantation, each ampler than the former. He declared
> that the Protestant religion was false; that the Catholic
> religion was the only true one; that he now believed in
> all the doctrines of the Catholic Church; that he had
> been a horrid blasphemer against the sacrament; that he
> was unworthy of forgiveness; that he prayed the People,
> the Queen and the Pope to have pity on, and to pray for
> his wretched soul; and that he had made and signed this
> declaration without fear, and without hope of favor, and
> for the discharge of his conscience, and as a warning to
> others.

He proclaimed his joy at returning to the Catholic Faith; he asked for and received sacramental absolution; and he partici-pated in the Mass.

It soon became clear, however, that Mary Tudor would not be moved. Recanters were usually pardoned, as the members of Parliament had been, "but now it was resolved that Cranmer's crimes were so enormous that it would be unjust to let him es-cape." The memory of his several previous "changes of heart" must surely have factored in as well.

Brought, therefore, to the public reading of his recantation, on his way to the stake; seeing the pile ready, now finding that he must die, and carrying in his breast all his malignity undiminished, he recanted his recantation, thrust into the fire the hand that had signed it, and thus expired, protesting against that very religion in which, only nine hours before, he had called God to witness that he firmly believed!

So far in the course of our story of bad shepherds, we've seen a man go from layman to pope in a single day; we've seen Roman popes and Avignon popes excommunicating one another; we've seen three popes at once during the Great Schism.

But it remained until the Reformation of the sixteenth century to show four, five, ten popes at once, scattered over Europe—and each now with a church of his own to lord it over, yet still unable to leave off quarrelling and anathematizing! And every one of them a Catholic to begin with.

Is it possible that even here, in this waking nightmare, the Catholic laity thrived? Most people know, after all, that Mary Tudor did not keep her throne; that her sister Elizabeth, in fact, instituted a general persecution of Catholics the likes of which had not been seen since before Constantine.

It depends, I suppose, on your definition of *thriving*. If *thriving* means keeping your possessions, your freedom, your untroubled lifestyle, then no, Catholic laymen did not thrive during the sixteenth and seventeenth centuries. *But many of them did earn crowns*—as promised by the apostles: "Blessed is the man who endures trial, for when he has stood the test he will receive the crown of life which God has promised to those who love him" (James 1:12). Many of their names, in fact, have been raised to the altar: St. Margaret Clitherow, St. Philip Howard, St. John Rigby, Bl. Richard Langhorne — and more than five hundred others when faithful clergy are included.

Let us ask their prayers during this, another difficult period in the life of our Holy Church. Working, praying, teaching, and striving against the abuses of our own times may offer us crowns, too.

Chapter 5

The Infamous Monster:
The Church That Surrendered to France

Sometimes the dam must break before the logjam can be cleared —and thus it was with the great Protestant revolt. Luther and the rest accomplished very little on the positive side of the ledger beyond this. Their alleged reforms, for the most part, proceeded on the principle of that celebrated farmer who burned down his own barn to get rid of the rats. The abuses that originally inspired the Protestant movement—simony, papal immorality, the sale of indulgences, and so forth—went untouched while the putative reformers changed doctrines, not practices, and then began to fight among themselves over that. Any prospect that Calvin, Zwingli, or one of the others might eventually win all of Protestantism, much less the whole Church, to his system was soon lost forever, along with any hope that the Reformation might live up to its name.

They had gained their independence (from any authority higher than that of their own secular princes, that is, who hereafter ruled as rigidly as any pope) and earned a fresh start inside their own borders, nothing more. But for those still striving to amend the Church of their fathers, Luther's dynamite, ironically, turned out to be the shock that finally did the trick.

The term *Counter-Reformation* is misleading, according to historian Henri Daniel-Rops: "It cannot rightly be applied, logically or chronologically, to that sudden awakening as of a startled giant, that wonderful effort of rejuvenation and reorganization, which in a space of thirty years gave to the Church an altogether new appearance."[50]

Suddenly, reformers within the Catholic fold got the traction that had always eluded them before. Dozens of vigorous religious orders were created—the Ursulines, the Capuchins, the Oratorians, the Somascan Fathers, the Discalced Carmelites, and, of course, the Jesuits—and these instantly began to make a difference. They lived chastely and austerely. They fed the hungry, instructed the ignorant, counseled the doubtful, admonished the sinner ... and made history.

Remedial catechesis, for both clergy and laity, was emphasized; genuine gospel preaching—such as that of the great St. Francis de Sales—was reinstated; scandalous priests were sent back to the bishop. And when, after nearly unbelievable difficulties, a great reforming synod was held—the Council of Trent—the pace was accelerated.

Evil-living clerics were removed; political appointments abolished; pluralism and absenteeism on the part of the episcopacy became an unpleasant memory from the past.

The rebirth was very real. It refreshed and renewed, but it was not actually the Millennial Dawn or the new Golden Age. It was, instead, the necessary building up for more dark times ahead.

Most of us today think of France as a Catholic country, but the issue was very much in doubt for a long while. Calvin, you

---

[50] Henri Daniel-Rops. "The Catholic Reformation," taken from the Fall 1993 issue of *The Dawson Newsletter*.

may recall, was a Frenchman himself; and from Geneva he encouraged his movement inside his home country. France, in fact, became the battleground of the Reformation — literally. The Wars of Religion (1562–1598) that broke out there amount to a violent thirty-five-year attempt on the part of the French Calvinists (known as Huguenots) to do to their country what Luther had done to the German Reich.

Rather like the long conflict in Vietnam, this one ended up as a proxy war between two larger outside blocs, with both the Catholic and Protestant powers supplying ever increasing infusions of foreign money and manpower. When it ended as a drawn battle, the Huguenot districts were partitioned into a smaller, seemingly permanent state within the state. Afterward, the French crown felt humiliated by the stalemate, much as America did after Vietnam, and its prestige abroad was greatly diminished.

Our next bad shepherd, Armand Jean du Plessis (better known as Cardinal Richelieu — yes, the bad guy from *The Three Musketeers*), drank deeply from his country's cup of humiliation. He lost his father to the Wars of Religion and began to gear up for further trouble at the age of fourteen, training as a military officer. It almost seems a shame to put Richelieu in the same class as monsters like Cranmer and Benedict IX: Richelieu's character appears to have been no worse and perhaps a little better than any other typical European statesman of the day; in fact, he became the first bishop in France to support quick implementation of the Tridentine decrees.

But his relentless, calculating determination to put France back on top, whatever the cost — even to the Catholic Faith — achieved long-term results as ugly as any of the others. Nationalism, in other words, took the driver's seat completely at this point; and Cardinal Richelieu, by surrendering to it so absolutely, took the first steps toward the great conflagration that almost destroyed Christian civilization outright in the twentieth century—the two cataclysmic world wars.

The trouble that young Armand sought to meet halfway came in spades. Almost as terrible in its own day as the world wars, the *Thirty Years' War* that began just as he came to power was the most destructive conflict Europe had seen thus far, resulting in over eight million casualties before all was said and done.

It started, you will not be surprised to learn, as more strife between Catholic and Protestant factions, this time within the fragmented Holy Roman Empire. Gradually, however, it devolved into a more straightforward recap of our old rivalry from the days of the Avignon papacy—the French crown versus the German emperors, struggling for continent-wide domination. Richelieu was instrumental in this transformation. When Louis XIII made the cardinal his first minister in 1624, Richelieu began to undermine the German cause by any means necessary, fair or foul.

When he saw the Spanish (allied to the Holy Roman emperors) about to take Northern Italy, Cardinal Richelieu made a fast alliance with the Swiss Protestants of Grisons—and helped them drive out the pope's own garrisons. He also directed subsidies and other aid to the Protestant princes of Sweden and Holland, to anyone whose cause, that is, might work to hinder the (Catholic!) emperors in some fashion. Like a football punted much farther downfield, this policy wound up permanently confirming the independence of a Protestant North Germany.

Domestically, Cardinal Richelieu acted to suppress Protestantism. He did this, paradoxically, by eliminating the legally protected enclave that had been carved out for them at the end of the previous wars. The principle the cardinal employed was a new one—that of freedom of religion for all and perfect equality under the law for Catholic and Protestant alike—so that the changes did not result, as you might expect, in persecutions or exile. Instead, the move put the disproportionately rich and privileged Huguenots on the same footing with everyone else, making them suddenly a mere minority. Thus, the French king gained his freedom from their growing, money-based ability to interfere with his actions. The corresponding fact that the Huguenots were now free to spread their settled hatred for Catholicism among the whole people and eventually become the basis of a new, anti-Catholic ruling class was a problem for another day.

Please don't misunderstand: Cardinal Richelieu thought Catholicism was good for the health of a nation and Protestantism bad. This is exactly why he acted to build up Catholicism within France—and to encourage Calvinism everywhere else. For Richelieu, there was only one question to be asked about any proposal: Is it good for the French or bad for the French?

He valued the Catholic Faith, but only as a means to an end. And if this meant putting France on strained terms with the popes (whose ostensible task, after all, was to nurture Catholicism everywhere), well, France had certainly found herself on the outs with a pope or two before now.

Who knew? Perhaps future popes might learn to see things his way, might even take a mind to visit their old haunts at Avignon again—only for a short stay, of course.

When the war was over, France was just where Armand Jean du Plessis always hoped she someday would be—standing atop the rubble as the most powerful nation in Europe. Though Richelieu himself had not actually survived to see it, the supremacy of the Hapsburg emperors was broken for the foreseeable future, leaving France to fill the vacuum. But the victory, as we will see, came at a steep price.

As the cardinal's policy shows, one of the main principles that created Protestantism had crept into Catholic thinking as well. Europe was no longer Christendom, not even in the minds of Catholics. All hope of restoring her lost unity faded after the Treaty of Westphalia—which had, to be sure, ended the war, but only by putting up an iron curtain between a recognized Protestant North and Catholic South Europe. Now national concerns were free to trump international Catholicity everywhere.

In theory, the Protestant princes of Sweden, Holland, Switzerland, and Germany's Lutheran states had achieved absolute control over religious matters in their own lands; but in reality, they were still subject to the vicissitudes of doctrinal opinion that roiled their fanatical populations. Henry VIII, on the other hand, had almost one-upped them by taking control of the Church in England *without really changing England's religion*. It was an extremely suggestive experiment—one that, as soon became apparent, even Catholic rulers had been watching with envy.

The mighty Sun King, Louis XIV, came to the throne of France in 1643. Thanks, in large part, to Cardinal Richelieu's efforts, his secular power was nearly unlimited—he was the most absolute ruler Europe had seen since the Caesars. He severely curtailed the power of his nobles. He cemented his popularity by instituting economic measures that created an unprecedented boom. And then, increasingly, Louis began to assert Henry-like privileges over the French Church as well. He sought and acquired the right to nominate bishops in France, then the power to sign off on papal decrees before allowing them to be published. His plan, according to Fr. John Laux, was to isolate the French Church, as far as he could from the Papacy. Nor were the people scandalized at his proceedings, for the worship of the Sovereign was one of their most cherished instincts. Louis supported Pope and bishops as long as they took their marching orders from him; if they refused, he was perfectly ready to make war on the one and to send the others to the Bastille.[51]

"The goal," as Bokenkotter adds, "was a tight union of Church and state, with the Church reduced to the junior partner."[52] The new policy came to be called *Gallicanism*—a French church for Frenchmen.

When the popes grew restive, Louis ordered his court theologians to reexamine some of the old theories about the limits of papal power that Thomas More once dallied with—and then rejected, at the cost of his head. Eventually, in 1681, Louis's infamous *Four Articles* were drawn up:

1. The pope may not interfere with the temporal concerns of princes.
2. A general council is superior to the pope in spiritual matters.
3. The rights and customs of the Gallican Church are inviolable.
4. The pope is not infallible, even in matters of faith, unless his judgment is confirmed by the consent of the whole Church.

Louis sent his Four Articles to the Sorbonne (the great University of Paris) whose professors, of course, rubber-stamped them

---

[51] Laux, *Church History*, 508.
[52] Bokenkotter, *A Concise History*, 242.

quickly. Afterward, the King ordered them taught in the seminaries as official doctrine; no priest could be ordained thereafter without affixing his signature as well.

As several of these matters had yet to be explicitly defined for the whole Church—the infallibility of the pope, for instance, didn't become dogma until 1870—the articles weren't *quite* heretical. One of the sponsors, in fact, was a man of great piety and many Christian virtues, the illustrious preacher Jacques-Bénigne Bossuet—only accidentally a bad shepherd. He seems to have lent his prestige to the effort out of a misguided zeal for the reunion of French Protestants and Catholics, the notion being that a papacy thus circumscribed might clear the way back for those who had been outraged by previous scandals.

The sitting pope—quiet, scholarly Innocent XI—would have none of it, however. Though not temperamentally combative by nature, Innocent saw right away that a line was being crossed. He condemned the Four Articles and pronounced them null and void, in France or anywhere else. He also ordered the awesome Sun King to stop stealing Church property (from the day he was crowned, Louis had been annexing old monasteries and appropriating diocesan revenues like a regular Henry VIII).

The French Church came very, very close to schism at this time, a split that would probably, like the English one, have hardened into permanence, in time transforming France, the very heart and soul of high medieval Christendom, into a Protestant country. The pope backed up his condemnation by refusing to confirm the ordination of any future clergy who had set their hand to the articles; Louis responded by henceforth nominating *only* Gallican bishops for the pope's approval. Soon, there were nearly forty vacant sees in France.

Finally, Louis became angry and threatened Italy with invasion. He reasserted French control over Avignon once more — a not-so-subtle signal about how Louis might ultimately choose to settle the matter if pushed. Innocent held fast, however, and just as importantly, resisted his very strong urge to excommunicate the king of France. Louis, too, stopped just short of a decisive break, a choice that many commentators believe resulted from a deepening personal faith on his part with the approach of old age.

Pope Innocent died before the matter was resolved, but his principled stand won out in the end. Military reverses during the 1680s sobered Louis up, it seems; and in 1693, he felt the need for reconciliation. He wrote to the new pope and offered a compromise: the king would continue to nominate candidates for the episcopacy but would no longer require them to affirm the Four Articles. The Gallican bishops expressed, at Louis's insistence, their regret for having taken part in the assembly that created the document, and in return, Innocent XII confirmed them to their sees.

Louis did not promise, however, that the Gallican principles themselves would be repudiated; indeed, Bossuet continued teaching them and lending them his enormous prestige. Seminarians were no longer required to believe them, but most of them did anyway, since the theories behind the articles continued to be taught approvingly for the next hundred years.

This left members of the Jesuit Order, based on principles of personal loyalty to the successor of Peter, the odd men out during the period ahead — and, in fact, put them firmly into the crosshairs. It also left other, more traditional Catholics, both inside France and out, to ponder the same question we do when examining the era today: *With Catholics like Richelieu, Louis, and Bossuet, who needs Protestants?*

By the time of our American Revolution, the Church in Europe had reached the low point of her prestige. She was still ubiquitous, still intertwined with civil society everywhere that Protestantism had not supplanted her. In France, the Church "formed virtually a state within the state and controlled all education and public relief; its parish priests were the sole registrars of births, marriages, and deaths; and its officials had power of censorship over publications deemed harmful to faith and morals."[53]

Yet, to many Frenchmen, the Church had begun to seem more and more superfluous, a mere relic from bygone centuries. Hostile observers exaggerated her faults, of course; but there was still plenty of holy living everywhere. There were many real saints; and most of the old issues from pre-Reformation days had been vigorously addressed. Even Voltaire, the popular new anti-Catholic pundit, was willing to concede that the nuns who ran French hospitals were doing praiseworthy work.

Yet good men, as well as the bad, were wondering whether the Church was, by this point, taking more than she paid back. By 1789, the Catholic Church in France owned as much as 10 percent of all the property in the country, with annual revenues approaching 150 million livres. It paid no direct taxes on this property yet still collected the annual tithe: one-tenth the value of all agricultural production.

What was all this paying for? The most visible indicator was the obvious wealth of the higher clergy, a class that overlapped completely with the French aristocracy and shared, to a great extent, in its decadent lifestyle. No bishop, nevertheless, nor even ordinary priests, paid any personal tax—nor could they be called up for military service. Clergymen accused of crimes could

[53] Ibid., 249.

be tried only in Church courts—tried, in other words, by their fellow clergy. Bad shepherds still turned up regularly, and when they did, the enemies of the Church spread the news widely by means of newspapers and other improved eighteenth-century communications.

The principles of Gallicanism—stronger than ever and now filtered down to the general public—suggested that the French government might call a reforming council of its own, with or without the pope's okay. When, in 1789, a major financial crisis broke with a shock like our Crash of 1929, the whole concept of "the French government" began to be transformed. Now, while poor, ordinary people continued to be taxed heavily, the luxuries of the nobility and the exemptions enjoyed by their friends, the "idle" clergy (and far too many of them really were idle), began to seem monstrous. In an effort to solve the crisis, King Louis XVI was prevailed upon to allow an assembly to convene, called the Estates General—a body that eventually brushed him aside and took matters into its own hands. Suddenly, and with very little thought beforehand, the *French Revolution* was under way.

A new congress, the National Assembly, met and quickly recommended measures that dramatically challenged the existing state of affairs.

As with all areas of French life, such a reform was long overdue, as the clergy themselves were ready to admit. Nor was there repugnance at the idea of the state undertaking such a reform—it seemed a logical corollary of the union of Church and state. Moreover, many of the reforms proposed were obvious and well thought out: The parasitic chapters attached to cathedrals were swept away; pastors were at last to be given a decent income;

and new and logical parochial and diocesan boundaries were drawn up.[54]

The longer the Assembly sat, however, the longer its wish list grew: the abolition of the mandatory tithe; the sale of most Church lands; the reduction and, in some cases, outright dissolution of monastic orders; and the end of payments to any foreign power (e.g., the papacy at Rome).

Perhaps surprisingly, the clergy cooperated with these early steps; they had, in fact, sided with the commoners from the beginning—the Third Estate, as it was called—against the nobles and the king, when the prospect of a National Assembly was first raised. Keenly sensitive to their current unpopularity and sincerely worried about the nation's looming bankruptcy, the Church surrendered her privileges willingly—even acquiesced, as Mary Tudor had done, in the confiscation of her property.

Nor was the Assembly at first especially hostile toward the Church per se; in fact, the delegates renewed the government's longstanding recognition of Catholicism as the official religion of the nation. But the thing had acquired a life of its own by this point: "Feeling themselves the vanguard of a European crusade, the Revolutionaries hoped to build a society that would be more efficient, more humane, and more orderly than the old order was."[55]

Early in 1790, the Revolution shifted into a higher gear. Nothing done so far had been insurmountable. No actual article of faith was under attack, and most of the encroachments might have been patiently endured for a long time without compromise.

[54] Ibid., 250.
[55] Ibid.

But now a series of fatal missteps redirected a revolution built on ideals of reason and enlightenment onto a path of almost unbelievable fanaticism and irrational frenzy.

The nobles had already been stripped of their titles; now the government of the Church was to be made subject to democracy as well. The newly minted Civil Constitution of the Clergy stipulated that bishops and priests were now to be elected locally, by electors who might be Protestants, Jews, even atheists—anyone chosen for the job by the revolutionary government and sworn to uphold its principles. The pope would be informed of the result but not asked for his blessing.

The newly appointed would then be required before ordination to swear a solemn oath "to be loyal to the nation, the law, and the king, and to support with all his power the constitution decreed by the National Assembly and accepted by the king." Notice the ghost of Gallican absolutism hovering over this supposedly democratic decree: the laws and the constitution must be obeyed with all one's power, while the pope rates only a memo. Did the revolutionaries quite realize what they were demanding? Taken literally, this oath required every priest in France to put his loyalty to the nation—*to the National Assembly of the revolution*—ahead of his loyalty to the Church, his loyalty to God.

To take the oath was to renounce obedience to the successor of Peter, to admit publicly that, for a French clergyman, no authority higher than the government at the Tuileries in Paris existed on earth. It was, for the conscientious, an invitation to self-excommunication.

Fifty percent took the oath immediately, on the spot. The other half delayed, waiting to hear from Pope Pius VI in Rome. The king decided to wait as well, even though it endangered his crown. Any resistance at all to the new "reforms" was already beginning to be read as hostility to the revolution, the voice of the people.

Those who took the oath justified themselves with the memory of Louis's grandfather, the Sun King. There was, after all, nothing in the Civil Constitution of the Clergy he would not have approved with pleasure; and the pope who finally compromised with him had declined in the end to condemn its underlying principles. Therefore, Pius, too, they reasoned, might ultimately yield. Saintly old Bossuet would have signed—also a very comforting thought to the signers.

It must also be conceded that a good many of those who complied were happy to see a potential split with Rome. They had long ago reconciled themselves to the idea that the French clergy was simply a branch of the civil service; and Huguenot ideas of independence and the private interpretation of Scripture had penetrated the ruling class deeply enough to transform many of them, already, into cynical atheists somehow retaining a religious income.

The other 50 percent—which included, we are happy to report, all but seven of the bishops so far—held out for the sovereignty of the Church. But even many of these secretly hoped the pontiff would cave in the end and bail them out. As the delay grew dangerously long, Cardinal Étienne-Charles de Loménie tried to provide cover by suggesting the holdouts might sign with "mental reservations"—a fancy name for deceit and hypocrisy.

Finally, Louis XVI himself could procrastinate no longer; on December 26, 1790, he granted his public assent to the Civil Constitution, allowing the oaths to become legally mandatory—at which point, up to 80 percent of the clergy in urban areas signed.

When Pope Pius finally did decide that the oath was impossible, he effectively transformed the signers into schismatics and the objectors into outlaws. The revolutionaries took countermeasures against "refractory priests" right away, barring them from public preaching and from performing baptisms and weddings and allowing them to continue in their churches only until suitable replacements could be found. Other than that, no open persecution took place—until events elsewhere conspired to cast the faithful priests in an uglier light.

First, the papal legate across the border in Germany told refugee aristocrats just what they wanted to hear: that the revolution was now godless and evil and the rest of Europe ought to rise up and put it down before it spread elsewhere.

The paranoia this news created in the minds of revolutionary leaders turned the legate's loose talk into a self-fulfilling prophecy. The Assembly quickly passed a law to create a twenty-thousand-man army to defend the borders—and Louis vetoed it. He had, in other words, sided with foreigners.

Not long afterward, the king—now seeing clearly where all this was going—attempted to flee with his family into Austria, where his brother-in-law Leopold ruled as archduke. The escape was foiled, however, and Louis was brought back to Paris. This had a profound effect on public opinion, since it was interpreted, once again, as conspiracy on the part of the king with counterrevolutionary, anti-French forces—including the sympathetic pope of Rome. Thus, the priests became potential traitors by extension.

Alarmed, Leopold, along with King Frederick William II of Prussia, issued an ill-timed statement declaring his intention to help the French king to "consolidate the basis of a monarchical government."[56] Then the revolutionaries, their paranoia proved

---

[56] Noah Shusterman, *The French Revolution. Faith, Desire, and Politics* (London: Routledge, 2014), chap. 4.

out, responded by pretty much declaring war on the rest of Europe—not only Austria and Prussia but Great Britain and the Dutch Republic. In April 1792, French armies invaded the Austrian Netherlands (what is today Belgium and Luxembourg) and somehow conquered them, to mad shouts of joy at home. The invasion had the effect of solidifying the nation's somewhat shaky support for the revolution in a way nothing else could have.

The crowned heads of Europe responded in kind: the kings of Portugal and Naples, the Grand Duke of Tuscany, and the Holy Roman emperor now declared war on revolutionary France.

After this, nothing was too bad for "disloyal" priests. Like the random Japanese Americans rounded up at the start of World War II, all of them were seen as tainted somehow and likely to betray their homeland. By the middle of 1792, thirty to forty thousand had been deported, many to hellholes such as the penal colony at French Guiana, and the death penalty was sanctioned for any who might dare to return.

Once the king himself was executed for treason on January 17, 1793, the wheels came completely off. The Prussian army, under the Duke of Brunswick, entered France and marched on Paris. This set off a panic that led to the infamous September Massacres, a wave of murders during which enraged mobs entered the jails containing political prisoners and killed more than a thousand of them in their cells, for fear that they might be released by the invading Prussians and join their ranks. Most of the victims had been among the nonjuring priests, those who would not sign the Civil Constitution. All told, 3 bishops and more than 220 priests lost their lives.

Whether frustration at the abuses metastasized under pressure into hatred for the Faith or whether it merely revealed a hidden hatred that had been present all along is hard to say. Either way, it now became all too apparent that the revolutionists intended to liquidate Catholicism in France.

Jacobins such as Jean-Paul Marat and Maximilien Robespierre, representing the hard left of the revolution, took up the cry Voltaire had popularized among the intelligentsia three decades earlier: "*Ecrasez L'Infame!*" (Crush the infamous thing!) "You are content with despising a monster which you ought to abhor and destroy," he had written in a series of letters to masons and other freethinkers. "Overthrow the Colossus!"

And now the effort was really made. A new republican calendar was minted with ten-day weeks, so that Sundays and holy days might be lost to memory. Yes, Christmas was abolished—as if by some silly villain in a TV special. The people were forbidden to put crosses on the graves of their loved ones. Statues and bells were melted down, and chalices and patens were seized for the gold they contained, as in England during Henry VIII's reign. Women were directed henceforth to name their infants after revolutionary heroes, not Christian saints. Propagandists resurrected every horror story you have read in this book—the Cadaver Synod, Benedict IX's bribery, John XXIII's incest—to justify joining the ranks of Christ's persecutors. The acts of the bad shepherds became an excuse for slaughtering the sheep.

The final nightmare, as we approach the climax to our story, is perhaps the worst of all. Government suppression of the Catholic Faith simply did not play in many areas of the country. Two regions in particular—the Vendée and the city of Lyons—revolted against the revolution. The Vendée, which had been blessed throughout the years with an unusually healthy and dedicated clergy, balked when told to conscript three hundred thousand men for the revolutionary army; they chose, rather, to create a

"Royal and Catholic Army" of their own, fighting "above all for the reopening of their parish churches with their former priests." Meanwhile, Lyons, too—the home of great supporters of the revolution in its early stages—felt the radical new Convention had gone too far and attempted a secession of its own. Both groups put up a valiant fight with very limited resources but ultimately failed.

With foreign armies pressing on all sides, economic collapse imminent, and now internal rebellion as well, the revolutionary leaders instituted their famous *Reign of Terror*. And while Madame Guillotine was addressing the problem of the aristocracy, three men were deputized to deal with the unwilling clergy and their misguided followers: General Louis Marie Turreau to the Vendée; Joseph Fouché to the rebels at Lyons; and Jean-Baptiste-Joseph Gobel, the archbishop of Paris, to address similar problems in the capital.

General Turreau was directed by the Committee of Public Safety to carry out a complete "pacification" of the Vendée, by which was meant, as their letters prove, a policy of total physical destruction. Beginning in December 1793, the general's troops burned villages, set fire to the surrounding forests, plowed crops under, and salted the fields afterward. Between thirty and fifty thousand civilians were massacred, regardless of age, sex, or political affiliation. Women carrying "counterrevolutionary babies" were particularly targeted. Bl. Guillaume Repin was among the victims, along with ninety-eight other religious and clergy, many of whom have since been beatified.

Citizen Fouché had made "dechristianization" his specialty. He reached Lyons in November 1793, ready to carry out reprisals against "the Whites" (the color of the royalist flag), which they would not soon forget. He ransacked churches, looted the sacred vessels, had nuns raped—all the usual atrocities. But Fouché was much more creative than General Turreau. He forced priests to apostatize so that they could assist him in desecrating sacred spaces. He began by using one of the churches to celebrate an obscene festival in honor of the Goddess of Reason. He then ordered signs painted and hung over the gates to every Catholic cemetery: "Death is an eternal sleep." Afterward, he employed a battery of two thousand battle-hardened troops to punish anyone even rumored to have given encouragement to the recent rebellion.

> On 4 December, 60 men, chained together, were blasted with grapeshot on the *plain de Brotteaux* outside the city, and 211 more the following day. Grotesquely ineffective, these mitraillades resulted in heaps of mutilated, screaming, half-dead victims, who were finished off with sabers and musket fire by soldiers physically sickened at the task.[57]

When this method proved too slow, a guillotine was set up and more traditional firing squads were set to work.

> Alas, Fouché's enthusiasm had proved a little too effective, for when the blood from the mass executions in the center of Lyons gushed from severed heads and bodies into the streets, drenching the gutters of the Rue Lafont, the vile-smelling red flow nauseated the residents, who irately complained to Fouché and demanded payment for damages. Fouché, sensitive to their outcry, obliged them

---

[57] David Andress, *The Terror: The Merciless War for Freedom in Revolutionary France* (New York: Farrar, Straus, and Giroux, 2005), 237.

by ordering the executions moved out of the city to the Brotteaux field, along the Rhône.[58]

The butchery continued for four months, well into the spring of 1794. When he was criticized for it later, even by some of the other Jacobins who began calling him "the Executioner of Lyons," Fouché justified his conduct: "We are causing much impure blood to flow, but it is our duty to do so, it is for humanity's sake.... The blood of criminals fertilizes the soil of liberty and establishes power on sure foundations."[59]

Archbishop Gobel was the bad shepherd called to put his stamp on all of this and to assist in dechristianization in his unique way. One of the "constitutional priests" (the ones who signed right away), Gobel kept on the good side of the revolution — and, indeed, earned his many promotions — by his eager willingness to make anticlerical statements and to support whatever anti-Christian measure was next on the docket. Whether he was cheerfully signing away a magnificent abbey, or agreeing to abolish the requirement for clerical celibacy, Archbishop Gobel was a steady source of comfort to his faithless and cowardly presbytery.

Finally, on November 7, 1793, he made his most significant contribution to national apostasy: he stood up before the National Convention and "courageously" resigned his episcopal office, insisting that he had done so out of love for the French people and through respect for their wishes. It was later revealed that he had been awakened by deputies during the previous night and told to resign or be killed. The remaining Paris churches were closed

---

[58] Ibid.
[59] Alan Schom, *Napoleon Bonaparte* (New York: HarperCollins, 1997), 253–255.

immediately; Gobel was henceforth the public face of revolutionary religious policy.

Yes, the Catholic archbishop of Paris was asked to sign off on the horrors of Lyons and the Vendée, and rather than die in torments himself, he willingly set his hand to the instrument. Here, finally, is the bottom of our very deep sewage barrel—thanks be to God!

Now out of a job, and following the example of their captain, most of the remaining "constitutional clergy" abruptly laicized themselves—and most of them quickly took wives as concrete proof of their defection. More than four thousand priests, in fact, married, while the total number who, like the archbishop, renounced their orders is closer to twenty thousand. A good number of them became active, bitter dechristianizers who willingly assisted Fouché and the rest in horrific sacrilege. Most of the others drowned their shame in drink and gave themselves over to the fashionable new debauchery.

Like most traitors, they were despised perhaps most of all by the very people who engineered their fall. Not long afterward, the revolution grew tired of fooling with them and packed them all off to Devil's Island anyway, along with the others.

Archbishop Gobel stayed around long enough to see Maximilien Robespierre, primary architect of the Great Terror, desecrate Notre Dame Cathedral by conducting a ceremony there inaugurating a new religion, founded by himself to replace the one Christ founded. Robespierre called it "the Cult of the Supreme Being," dedicated to the impersonal, clockmaker god of Deism.

> In attempts to destroy Catholicism, the dechristianizers did not intend to leave a religious vacuum, for they still shared the *ancien régime*'s principle that no state could

survive without a public religion.... His [Robespierre's] new liturgy was inaugurated on a beautiful day in June 1794, with himself as high priest: Dressed in a sky-blue coat, his hair carefully powdered, he led a procession from the Tuileries bearing a bouquet of berries, grain, and flowers. The people sang republican hymns, and after a sermon, Robespierre ignited an artfully made cardboard figure labeled Atheism; it crumpled, and then out of its ashes stepped another figure representing Wisdom.[60]

Images of Christ and the saints had been cleared out beforehand. Similar events took place in the nation's other churches. The hysterical madmen did not even scruple to desecrate the relics of St. Joan of Arc, venerated by their fathers as the savior of France: "Her standard remained," lamented Mark Twain (himself no great friend of religion),

for three hundred and sixty years, and then was destroyed in a public bonfire, together with two swords, a plumed cap, several suits of state apparel, and other relics of the Maid, by a mob in the time of the Revolution. Nothing which the hand of Joan of Arc is known to have touched remains in existence except a few preciously guarded military and state papers which she signed, her pen being guided by her clerk or her secretary.[61]

Not long after this, the revolution expended its remaining force in destroying its own. Georges Danton, Marat, and Jacques Hébert were already gone; now Gobel and Robespierre were both

---

[60] Bokenkotter, *A Concise History*, 255.

[61] Mark Twain, *Joan of Arc* (San Francisco: Ignatius Press, 1988), 314–315.

guillotined during one final spasm of internal strife between the revolutionists themselves. Joseph Fouché was among those who engineered their downfalls.

The whole thing would have collapsed completely had not Napoleon Bonaparte, most successful of the revolutionary generals, risen to save everything that was worth saving. He did it, ironically, by rejecting all committees, all protracted debates about reason and the rights of man, and taking to himself a personal authority as absolute as Louis XIV's.

Though he, too, flirted with active anti-Catholicism—taking captive the aged pope who had blessed the armies that invaded France and inadvertently causing the pope's death—Napoleon soon saw plainly what the doctrinaires and the demagogues could not: the Catholic Faith was permanent and immovable in the hearts of his people. Making war against it was like trying to extinguish the sun. There was nothing inherently antireligious in the idea of a republican form of government; no article in the catechism against voting or the equality of all citizens before the law; nor any requirement that bishops must become officers of the state.

He remembered, as most had forgotten, that Catholics had supported the revolution in its earlier, purer form. To employ another analogy from more recent conflicts, Napoleon saw what so many German officers saw during World War II: that the party ideologues had become so obsessed with persecuting a powerless religious minority that they continued to expend on that effort, right up to the end, vital resources that were desperately needed on the battlefields to avert invasion.

At the peak of his power, therefore, Napoleon simply called the whole thing off. He summoned Cardinal Martiniana to his Italian headquarters and sent him on a mission: "Go to Rome and tell the Holy Father that the First Consul wishes to make him a gift of thirty million Frenchmen."

Here is our last, best example of a laity that stayed strong while so many of their shepherds turned bad. Under incredible pressure, in the sight of systematic horrors to make one doubt the very existence of God, the faithful held fast. The constitutional clergymen had been resisted everywhere; the national guard often had to be called when a new one arrived to take the place of a faithful man. Just as happened in the great Arian crisis of the fourth century, when another crafty minority had attempted a takeover that the people didn't want, most Frenchmen would not even receive the sacraments from priests appointed by the revolutionary assemblies. They preferred to meet underground, to hold fast until deliverance came.

Even so, they weren't, as their enemies pretended, true counterrevolutionaries, hardened defenders, that is, of the old abuses. Many of those, in fact, who had been angriest at the Church at the beginning eventually realized they were angry at the bad shepherds, not at the Faith itself.

And thus, a revolution undertaken on behalf of the poor and the defenseless (but actually run by work-shy dilettantes and philosophers) was wrecked by a courageous Catholic laity who just would not be tricked into deserting Christ out of anger with Judas.

Napoleon, it is true, was still every inch the Gallican. When, in a curious recapitulation of Charlemagne, Pope Pius VII crowned him emperor of the French in the very cathedral where Robespierre had celebrated profane rites just a few years earlier, Napoleon insisted on a concordat that still infringed greatly on the rights of the Church. The First Consul himself would nominate future bishops, though the pope was given the right of refusal; stolen property, as in England, would remain in the hands of strangers. Napoleon even insisted that Louis XIV's Four Articles still be taught in the seminaries. There were, in other words, struggles ahead. The Golden Age had not arrived, nor even the Millennial Dawn.

The conflict was not over.

The adventure continues, even for us today, and probably will till kingdom come.

Afterword

What can poor folk like you and me carry away from a train wreck like this? I said in my introduction that I wanted to provide some forewarning about the shepherd who ends up being a challenge to your faith; and also to offer a bit of historical perspective on our current crisis, not as a way to minimize it, but as a method for lessening that particular kind of shock that cripples and debilitates, causes despair and defeat.

I feel confident that I've accomplished both of these things, even at the risk of a faith-shattering rude awakening. Beyond those aims, however, I think there are still two kinds of lessons we can carry away from spectacles like this: the right kind and the wrong kind. Let's start with the wrong kind.

If your first reaction is to conclude that the Church stands revealed in these pages as a fraud, whose ugly underbelly cancels out all her pious pretentions — then you may have been laboring under false ideas about her mission all along.

If your main impression of the Church thus far has been that of a valuable institution in society, a club to which responsible people will choose to belong, or a quasi-ethnic heritage one ought to be true to; whose main purpose in the world is to instill family values and to provide charming festivals on holidays and solemn ceremonies at family high points, such as births, weddings, and teen graduations ... then revelations like these truly must seem monstrous.

But the Church is not and was never intended to be a society for keeping your kids safe or for enhancing civic order (however fruitful it might be in producing these side effects) — much less was it ever an association for improving other people's morals. As Jesus Himself said, "My kingship is not of this world" (John 18:36).

What, then, is it meant to be?

The Church is a beachhead at Normandy, a rescue mission against desperate odds, to save a remnant of fallen humanity out of the war zone called Earth.

The first few chapters of the Bible set the stage for the rest of the story: a world gone wrong early on, failed choices that left our whole race in bondage, a world with the devil in charge — "the god of this world" according to St. Paul, "the prince of the power of the air" (2 Cor. 4:4; Eph. 2:2) — which even God Himself will be able to save only by shedding His blood.

And our earliest lessons from the catechism should have alerted us to a lifelong struggle ahead:

> Our nature was corrupted by the sin of our first parents, which darkened our understanding, weakened our will, and left in us a strong inclination to evil.... The body is inclined to rebel against the soul, and the soul itself to rebel against God.... This corruption of our nature and other punishments remain in us after original sin is forgiven.[62]

The tone of the Christian story, then, is not that of an essentially happy world that just needs a little tweaking, where, if good

---

[62] *Baltimore Catechism*, qq. 259, 263, 267.

people will just behave and go to church as they should, all will be well.

No, the Bible leads us to expect a harrowing story in advance: a story with heroes and villains, yes, but also a story in which the heroes — like Saul and Judas — can go wrong and sometimes wind up as villains. In this story, even the best souls can stumble and fail to reach the finish line. The throne, for instance, on which our Savior sits was originally the throne of Saul, not David, lost through disobedience. And Judas Iscariot might have been one of the greatest of all apostles, might have written one or more books of our inspired New Testament, had he passed the test, had he stayed true. Ours is a world, then, where bad things can really happen, including that thing called failure and damnation — and not just to somebody else.

The revelations on display in this book, therefore — and the ones on the nightly news nowadays — are perfectly in line with *the kind of story this is*: a story with champions who crack, lookouts asleep in the crow's nest, soldiers who sometimes turn and run.

Are these aspects of the tale faith shattering?

In a sense, yes — they have the potential to make us lose heart. But that danger is much worse for someone who, to begin with, has naïve ideas about what is ahead, who might, for a while, like the bad shepherds themselves, have taken his eyes off the prize.

Another wrong reaction is a loss of perspective that can lead one to view the Church as actually *worse* than the world she is meant to save. Once again, the great G. K. Chesterton sharpens the focus for us:

> When people impute special vices to the Christian
> Church, they seem entirely to forget that the world

(which is the only other thing there is) has these vices much more. The Church has been cruel; but the world has been much crueler. The Church has plotted; but the world has plotted much more. The Church has been superstitious; but it has never been so superstitious as the world is when left to itself.[63]

We must compare apples with apples, in other words; compare the Catholic Church not with the ideal Church in our minds or with the Church Triumphant at the end of time, but with roughly similar institutions created to achieve similar goals. We must compare it with idealistic experiments such as Soviet communism, European colonialism, or the French Revolution. "The world will do all that it has ever accused the Church of doing," continues Chesterton,

> and do it much worse, and do it on a much larger scale, and do it (which is worst and most important of all) without any standards for a return to sanity or any motives for a movement of repentance. Catholic abuses can be reformed, because there is the admission of a form. Catholic sins can be expiated, because there is a test and a principle of expiation. But where else in the world today is any such test or standard found; or anything except a changing mood, [such as that] which makes patriotism the fashion ten years ago and pacifism the fashion ten years afterwards?[64]

---

[63] G.K. Chesterton, *All Things Considered* (London: Methuen, 1908), 277–278.

[64] *The Collected Works of G.K. Chesterton*, vol. 3 (San Francisco: Ignatius Press, 1986), 218–219.

In a world like ours, where whole generations are going mad scouring the Internet for some religion, for some nation, some movement that *doesn't* have an underbelly, where the shepherds never have gone wrong, which one might join without ever being embarrassed later, this is a valuable insight to remember. If we postpone lending our aid to humanity until we find some humans worthy of our association ... well, it's going to be a long wait, so bring a lunch.

The Church's sins are worse in one way only: that we ought to have known—and, in fact, did know—better. But that is, in its own way, a backhanded compliment, and one that can easily be fleshed out by going back to those "cotton candy" stories I deliberately left out of this volume—the staggering, self-sacrificing grace on display everywhere else in Church history.

For every pope or cardinal who went bad, there are ten at least who poured out their lives for my salvation and yours. If Judas Iscariot died by his own hand, the other eleven died for me and you—Peter crucified upside down, Nathanael skinned alive, Thomas speared to the ground by the jealous Brahmans of India. I do recommend, in other words, that you now follow this stiff shot of *Bad Shepherds* with a chaser such as *St. Leo the Great* or *The Life of St. Francis Xavier*. (Better yet, let me go ahead and suggest Mike Aquilina's inspiring book *Yours Is the Church*, for a balancing look at the bigger picture.)

Here's another lesson I'm hoping you won't carry away. If I have shown that popes are not above criticism, that one does not become a disloyal Catholic merely by acknowledging the possibility of serious papal malfeasance (and I think I have), I hope I *have not* lent any momentum to the pendulum swing that so often follows: i.e., that it's now open season on popes, who can be heckled with impunity from armchairs on the sidelines.

A Catholic's criticism of the Holy Father must always be the same kind of criticism we might be forced to aim at our own earthly fathers—reluctant, unenthusiastic, sad, and forbearing.

Snark, sarcasm, and snideness are not on St. Paul's list of the fruits of the Spirit. Even an ordinary parent who beats, betrays, drinks, and cheats will never be just *some guy* to us, some stranger to be jibed at for fun. He's our own father, such as he is. "If one curses his father or his mother, his lamp will be put out in utter darkness" (Prov. 20:20).

Individual popes certainly may, with some effort, alienate our affections eventually, may even drive us—as did Urban VI and John XII—to throw our hands up in resignation. But we must cling to our usual roles until the very last moment such an allegiance is compatible with our other Christian duties. We may take for our model that man for all seasons, St. Thomas More, who, even at the foot of the scaffold to which Henry sent him, was willing to confess: "I die the king's faithful servant, but God's first."

Now, the right kind of lessons. First, count your blessings! We can never minimize the horrors that victims of abuse have suffered, not only in our country but around the world. And the cover-ups, which do not seem even now to have ended, may almost be worse, since they are not the actions of a relatively small portion of depraved individuals but seem to reflect settled, ongoing policy on the part of otherwise respected prelates.

Nevertheless, we can at least thank God that the bad shepherds aren't beheading thousands of us at a time for protesting, or propping up mummies on the papal throne, or filling us full of grapeshot these days merely for wanting good priests back in our same old churches. In other words, it's not the end of the world. Or, if it is the end of the world (something we believers in the Parousia can never actually rule out), it's not because things have never been this bad before.

Second, we mustn't allow ourselves to become the man who burned down his barn to get rid of the rats. Strong emotions are valid here, even justified. They must be channeled into a constructive force, not allowed to crash undirected like a flash flood, as they were in Luther's day, destroying the good things along with the bad. A tantrum may feel good now, but there's always a mess to clean up afterward. We think, for instance, of our Lord's admonitions in the parable of the wheat and the weeds: "'Do you want us to go and root them out?' But the householder said, 'No; lest in gathering the weeds you root up the wheat along with them'" (see Matt. 13:28–29). And those who leave the Church at this hour are leaving it to her enemies. As Catholic commentator John Clark recently put it, "The Church Militant, like those who sought to restore liberty and justice to America, benefits little from summer soldiers and sunshine Catholics; it benefits much from those who seek to conquer the forces of hell, even and especially when those forces appear in the Catholic Church."

Finally, this story of the bad shepherds has taught us the slow, steady, but enormous power of God's blessed laity. In the planning stages of this book, I was asked a very searching question: "My understanding is that only a minority of today's Catholics know—much less hold to—most of the teachings of the Church. Can we really expect today's laity to be a good counterbalance to the failings of bad shepherds? If not, what can serve to right the barque of Peter and clean the Augean stables?"

My answer? Nothing. Nothing can.

It's like those who, in 1940, saw Hitler's terrifying armies on the march, looked around at a generation of playboys and jitterbugs, and wondered who besides these could stop him.

You and I, laypeople, have been nominated, ready or not. We are the plan. And if the odds seem long … well, they always have been, since David laid down his sword and picked up a sling instead.

The story of David and Goliath, in fact, may be the key — along with similar Bible lessons about the Walls of Jericho, about Gideon's three hundred, and about the rebuilding of Jerusalem after the Babylonian Captivity: "This is the word of the LORD to Zerubbabel: Not by might, nor by power, but by my spirit, says the LORD of hosts" (Zech. 4:6).

I said that the laity has enormous power. It's true — for God's Spirit is with them. But that power was never the strength of mere numbers, nor of stubbornness, persistence, or conservatism — not even righteous indignation. "For the anger of man does not work the righteousness of God" (James 1:20).

When we look for heroism in the story of the bad shepherds, we get much closer to the truth by saying that the laity who thought they lacked power were, by virtue of that very fact, protected from its corrupting influence.

What we have seen is a miracle of humility, a spiritual gift we do not want to relinquish in our own hour of trial.

There's another Belloc quote going around these days: "The Catholic Church is an institution I am bound to hold divine — but for unbelievers a proof of its divinity might be found in the fact that no merely human institution conducted with such knavish imbecility would have lasted a fortnight."[65] Boiled down to its main point, this saying is an affirmation that God has imbued His people with a miraculous unction of *endurance*, so that

---

[65] Remark to William Temple, quoted in Robert Speaight, *The Life of Hilaire Belloc* (London: Hollis and Carter, 1957), 383.

the members of Christ's Body don't evaporate even when goaded far beyond the normal limits of human stamina.

Nor is it too late for doubtful, poorly catechized, or previously casual Catholics to rise to the occasion, to rally themselves, overcome their handicaps, and save the Church of their fathers.

I suspect that many of those who rose up to throw out the Arians or stood up to Archbishop Gobel may very well have been "nominal Catholics" or even "cafeteria Catholics"—until the sufferings of the Church under bad shepherds stirred something dormant in their hearts, something put in there at their baptism. These, in fact, may prove by the end to have been our own most valuable reserves—and the greatest evidence that all our victories belong to the Lord.

Rootless, they stayed planted.

And who knows? Perhaps this most recent wave of sordid revelations will act as dynamite to the logjam once again. We must pray that it does—along with prayers of reparation, repentance, and abandonment to God's will.

"The arm of flesh will fail," said King Hezekiah, confronted by a vastly superior force of enemies. "Do not be afraid or dismayed before the king of Assyria and all the horde that is with him; for there is one greater with us than with him" (see 2 Chron. 32:7–8). "So lift your drooping hands," says the writer of the Letter to the Hebrews, "and strengthen your weak knees, and make straight paths for your feet, so that what is lame may not be put out of joint, but rather be healed" (12:12–13).

I don't have the secret reform scheme myself—but we can, I think, before parting company, gather a few broad tactics from these nasty stories I have forced you to root around in. The parishioners of the exiled Athanasius, for instance, "chose rather to be sick and to run the risk of going unbaptized than to permit the hand of the Arians to come upon their head." We, likewise, can empty the churches of known collaborators in the cover-up. Let them preach to vacant pews. We can receive our lessons and our sacraments elsewhere: an irregularity, to be sure, but these are irregular times.

The fourth-century Church also ran known reprobates out of town; and while I don't condone their use of tar and feathers these days, buildings that have been put up and paid for by the laity can have new locks installed; and yes, faithless priests can be sent back to the bishop.

Many church functions — many of the ones that have gone most neglected, in fact, such as remedial catechesis and adult formation — likewise do not require the hand of a sacerdotal minister. The men and women who returned Athanasius to his see prayed in their own homes long prayers for strength and deliverance, unassisted by clergy. We've heard talk about "the hour of the laity" for decades; now seems the time to make it more than talk.

Certainly we do have priests and bishops who want to help — but we don't need their permission. As enshrined in canon law, the laity,

> according to the knowledge, competence, and prestige which they possess, have the right and even at times the duty to manifest to the sacred pastors their opinion on matters which pertain to the good of the Church and to make their opinion known to the rest of the Christian faithful, without prejudice to the integrity of faith and morals, with reverence toward their pastors, and attentive to common advantage and the dignity of persons. (Canon 212.3)

Those times of duty have come. A time to purify the Church ourselves, a time to tell the clergy (reverently) to "lead, follow, or get out of the way."

All the crimes of Church history are raising their horrible heads again—politics in the Curia, unbelief among the clergy, unchastity in the seminaries and the monasteries, resistance to reform—and we the laity, a "Royal and Catholic Army" sworn to King Jesus, cannot go back to business as usual.

I mentioned repentance and reparation for the sins of others, the kind of talk that rankles many who were, of course, never involved in any such evil thing as child abuse. But if you've come this far in your Christian life without realizing that reparation for the sins of others is at the very center of our Holy Faith, as it is often centered above our altars in the image of the Crucifix, well, you really do need remedial catechesis.

But we do have actual sins of our own in this mess, sins that call out for sincere confession and penance.

Not sins of abuse, but of *tolerance*.

Nothing, after all, beyond additional detail, has really been added by these revelations of 2018, above what we learned in 2002, more than sixteen years ago—except that then, we wanted it all to be over quickly.

This time, we don't want it over; not until the rats are out of the barn with the barn still standing—so that we can all go back in it again to gather the harvest.

"For what is our hope or joy or crown of boasting before our Lord Jesus at his coming?" asked the apostle Paul, writing of his fellow clergy to the lay folk at Thessalonica. "*Is it not you? For you are our glory and joy!*" (1 Thess. 2:19–20).

About the Author

Rod Bennett is the author of *Four Witnesses: The Early Church in Her Own Words*, widely considered to be a modern classic of Catholic apologetics. His other works include: *The Apostasy That Wasn't; The Extraordinary Story of the Unbreakable Early Church*, and *Chesterton's America; A Distributist History of the United States*. His articles have appeared in *Our Sunday Visitor, Rutherford Magazine*, and *Catholic Exchange*; and he has been a frequent guest on EWTN and Catholic Answers radio. Rod lives with his wife and two children on the two-hundred-year-old family homeplace in the Great Smoky Mountains of East Tennessee.

Sophia Institute

Sophia Institute is a nonprofit institution that seeks to nurture the spiritual, moral, and cultural life of souls and to spread the Gospel of Christ in conformity with the authentic teachings of the Roman Catholic Church.

Sophia Institute Press fulfills this mission by offering translations, reprints, and new publications that afford readers a rich source of the enduring wisdom of mankind.

Sophia Institute also operates two popular online Catholic resources: CrisisMagazine.com and CatholicExchange.com.

Crisis Magazine provides insightful cultural analysis that arms readers with the arguments necessary for navigating the ideological and theological minefields of the day. *Catholic Exchange* provides world news from a Catholic perspective as well as daily devotionals and articles that will help you to grow in holiness and live a life consistent with the teachings of the Church.

In 2013, Sophia Institute launched Sophia Institute for Teachers to renew and rebuild Catholic culture through service to Catholic education. With the goal of nurturing the spiritual, moral, and cultural life of souls, and an abiding respect for the role and work of teachers, we strive to provide materials and programs that are at once enlightening to the mind and ennobling to the heart; faithful and complete, as well as useful and practical.

Sophia Institute gratefully recognizes the Solidarity Association for preserving and encouraging the growth of our apostolate over the course of many years. Without their generous and timely support, this book would not be in your hands.

www.SophiaInstitute.com
www.CatholicExchange.com
www.CrisisMagazine.com
www.SophiaInstituteforTeachers.org

Sophia Institute Press® is a registered trademark of Sophia Institute.
Sophia Institute is a tax-exempt institution as defined by the
Internal Revenue Code, Section 501(c)(3). Tax I.D. 22-2548708.